To Don!
Best Wishes!
Jerome Art

Also by Jerome Arthur

Antoine Farot and Swede
Down the Foggy Ruins of Time
Life Could be a Dream, Sweetheart
One and Two Halves
The Journeyman and the Apprentice
The Muttering Retreats
The Death of Soc Smith
The Finale of Seem
Oh, Hard Tuesday
Brushes with Fame

Got no Secrets to Conceal

A Novel

Jerome Arthur

Got no Secrets to Conceal

Published by Jerome Arthur
P.O. Box 818
Santa Cruz, California 95061

831-425-8818
JeromeArthurNovelist.com
Jerome@JeromeArthurNovelist.com

Acknowledgments

Special thanks to Nancy Krusoe for editorial assistance and to Sherri Goodman for the cover art.

One

I can't believe I got involved in such a sordid affair with a woman whose sexual exploits were legendary. At least the way she talked, they were legendary. She was married; I was engaged to be married.

It started one Friday in October when we had our first lunch date. That was when it started in earnest. It really started in January the year before that. I'd just finished my course of study in Administration of Justice at Cabrillo College and opened my own detective agency, Jack Lefevre Investigations. I ran the business out of my California bungalow on Center Street in downtown Santa Cruz.

I thought it might be a good idea to hone my craft by taking some Legal Studies classes at U.C. Santa Cruz. I wasn't very busy yet in my new trade, so I had plenty of time to spend taking the classes. Just for the fun of it, I also took a European Novel class. My interest in literature was sparked when I took some lit. classes at San José State when I was working on my B.A. degree in Spanish. I had this crazy idea that I was going to be a high school Spanish teacher, but by the time I graduated, there were no teaching jobs on the horizon, so I got a job as a checker at Safeway and joined the retail clerk's union. I did that for ten years, saving enough money to buy the bungalow and get my A.J. certification from Cabrillo.

Got no Secrets to Conceal

Renata Lowell was in the European Novel class. I didn't meet her in the class. The face-to-face meeting, in fact, happened on the bus going into town the first day of class. We were sitting next to each other.

"Are you in a European Novel class?" she asked.

I looked at her and saw a plain looking woman, no classic beauty, but definitely attractive. Her long brown hair was tied back. There was a streak of natural gray in front on the left, starting at the hairline on her forehead. Her eyes were two colors, the left one green, the right one amber, but the color wasn't the distinguishing feature. Her pupils had a flinty quality that seemed to spark when she smiled as though the flints were being struck by metal. She had a nice overbite that made her smile dazzle. Her body was slim and shapely.

"That's right," I said. "How'd yuh know?"

"You were sitting next to me in the class, and I saw that book," she said, pointing at the book I was reading. "It can't have anything to do with that class, can it?"

The book was John Gardner's *Nickel Mountain.*

"Right again."

"Are you reading it for another class?"

"No. This guy's a good writer. First one of his I've read. Think I'm go'n'a try to read 'em all."

"Really! I'm impressed. Why are you taking the novel class?"

"For fun. I already got a degree in Spanish. I got an A.J. certificate from Cabrillo, and I'm running a little detective agency outa' my house. What I'm taking seri-

7

ously up here is a legal studies class. I was in that class just before the lit. class.

And so the conversation went. It's amazing how much we talked about and how well we got to know each other on such a short bus ride. She was a twenty-nine-year-old re-entry student who had started college straight out of high school, and then dropped out at the end of her sophomore year. She was ten years younger than I and a Spanish lit. major, which, I realized straight away, was the first thing we had in common. When we got to Metro center, the bus terminal downtown, I gave her my business card, and we went our separate ways.

Back at my bungalow, there was a message on my answering device from Debra, my fiancé.

"Hi, honey," she said. "Wan'a go out to dinner tonight? It's three-thirty now. I'm just leaving school and should be getting home pretty soon. Can probably be at your place by five. Call me back. Let me know if you're up for it."

When I first met Debra, I thought she was the most beautiful woman I'd ever seen. She was five feet four inches tall and weighed a trim hundred and twenty-five pounds. Her blue eyes and dark brown hair contrasted beautifully with her light Irish complexion. She taught fifth grade at an elementary school in the Santa Cruz mountains and lived in a two-bedroom condo up in University Terrace on the westside. She and I had gotten engaged just as I was starting the program at Cabrillo a couple years ago. We'd been dating for five years before that, so we were serious about each other for some seven years. The plan was for me to move in with her after we

8

Got no Secrets to Conceal

got married, and I'd continue to run my business out of the bungalow on Center Street.

It was Monday afternoon, twenty to four. I must've just missed her call. I called her house.

"Hey, Babe," I said into the telephone after her greeting message ran. "Your plan for the evening sounds great. See yuh when yuh get here."

All those years together, we were as good as married, and being faithful to Debra, a classic beauty with a beautiful smile and brains, was easy. Not once in that time did I ever think about getting intimate with another woman. That was of absolutely no interest to me, completely absent from my thoughts, and then, from out of nowhere, Renata tossed out her proposition. It was more surprising because things like that never happened to me.

It started out innocently enough. We'd see each other when the class met, and we'd catch the bus together on those days for the rest of that winter quarter. She told me later that she was sending out signals on those bus rides, but I wasn't picking up on them. I could only remember one time when she repeated something a couple times that I thought could have been a signal, and that was when she complained about the lack of sex in her marriage.

I sat out the spring quarter and didn't take any classes until fall. It would be six months before I saw her again. That was one day as I waited for a bus to campus. Just as it approached and I stepped to the curb, I heard someone calling my name. When I looked up the street

Jerome Arthur

to see who it was, a very pregnant Renata waddled down the sidewalk in my direction.

"Are you catching this bus?" I asked when she got closer.

"Yes," she replied.

"Hold on," I told the driver as I put my foot on the first step. Then I waited for her to get there.

When we got to our seats, we got reacquainted. She was going up to campus to find out what classes she needed to graduate. She was sitting out this quarter and the next. Her baby was due in November, and she planned to take plenty of time off to spend with it. She hoped she'd only have four more quarters to go. I told her I was still a private eye and was taking another Legal Studies class that quarter.

We went our separate ways when we got to campus, and I didn't see her again for another nine months or so. It was one day in late spring as I was riding my bike on Beach Street. She approached from the opposite direction on the sidewalk. It had been so long since I'd seen her that I didn't recognize her at first.

"Hey, how're yuh doin'?" I asked when our eyes met. I pulled up to the curb.

"Fine. How are you? It's been a long time."

"Yes, it has been a long time. How've yuh been? How's your baby doin'?"

She looked like she'd gotten her body back in shape after her pregnancy and childbirth.

"The answer to both questions is fine. She's getting to be quite the little person. Six months old. You ought'a see her."

10

Got no Secrets to Conceal

"So, what're yuh doin' down in this neck a' the woods?"

From all the many conversations we'd had on bus rides, I knew she lived in Boulder Creek, nine miles away up Highway Nine. This seemed to me a little faraway to be just out walking.

"I've got this part-time job over here around the corner, and I was just taking a little break for a walk along the beach."

"Where do yuh work?"

"It's pretty low key. I work for a woman who lives up on Third Street. Kinda' like a personal assistant. Open her mail, pay her bills, balance her checkbook, get her stuff ready for the accountant at tax time. I got the job from an ad posted on the bulletin board in the placement office on campus. It's a nice little part-time thing. Flexible schedule and it pays five bucks an hour."

"'Sounds like a pretty good deal."

"Yes, it is. Say, has anyone ever told you that you look a lot like James Garner? You know, the actor?"

"Many times. He's a bit older'n I am and a bit taller, but yeah, a lot of people tell me that."

"Uncanny."

We chatted for about ten minutes, and for some reason, I decided I had to get going. I started to give her my card again, but she said she still had the other one I gave her the first day we met.

"I've driven up and down your street several times looking for your place and never could find it. You have a sign in the window or something?"

11

"Not really. I do have a very small plaque on my front door, but yuh got'a be on the porch to read it. Yuh know, I'm not even supposed to be doing business in the house. It's zoned residential. I'm kinda' practicing as a home business. Check out the address again, and then just come on by, but it's best to call first. Make sure I'm there. I come and go as I please. One a' the nice things about workin' for yourself. Gi'me a call. If I'm not there, you c'n leave your name and number on my answering service, and I'll get back to you within a couple hours. Come by sometime and we can go to lunch."

"I will," she said. "I'd love to go to lunch with you."

And we parted, but not before I said to her impulsively,

"Here, gi'me a hug," and she did.

It wasn't two minutes after she disappeared into the crowd that I realized I should've asked her what she was doing for lunch right then. *I* wasn't doing anything, just hanging around. It was only one o'clock, and I didn't have appointments scheduled that afternoon, and I really didn't have anything else to do. I turned around to look for her, but she was gone.

I peddled down to the river levee and on up to downtown and back home. I went into the kitchen and fixed myself a hot dog for lunch. When I finished eating, I went into my office and looked to see if there were any phone messages. I was hoping that Renata had left a message. Unfortunately, she hadn't.

The next time I saw her, I was taken completely by surprise. It was almost noon on a busy Friday in Au-

Got no Secrets to Conceal

gust. I was in my office talking to my future father-in-law, Charles Morrison. He and Debra's mom, Frances, lived in a condo development for retirees in San José. You had to be a Mason to live there. It was kind of like Paradise Park up on Highway Nine. He was asking me to look into one of his neighbors, who, he thought, wasn't a Mason. The guy was violating some of the association rules, and Charles wanted to get him out of there. The guy's father, who was a Mason, was the owner of record of the condo, and Charles was sure the kid wasn't a Mason.

Besides coming over to throw some business my way, the Morrisons were taking Debra and me out to lunch. Her mother was already up at her place waiting for her to get home from school. She was teaching a half day and was coming with her mother to meet us at Lily Marlene on the Mall.

It was a good thing we weren't meeting at my place because, before I knew it was happening, Renata walked through the door with a baby on her hip. She sat down in the chair closest to the front door. Her baby immediately squirmed off her lap and onto the floor. She crawled over to the bookcase along the wall and started pulling books off the shelves. Renata picked her up and sat down again with the baby on her lap. I went over and took her small hand and held it in mine.

"I remember you when you were inside your mother," I said to her. "How old is she now?" This to Renata.

"Nine months. She'll be a year old in November."

13

Jerome Arthur

"So, what're you up to?" I asked.

"We were just driving by when I saw your little place here and decided to stop and pay you a visit."

"All right! I'm glad you did, although I'm kinda' tied up right now and really can't visit."

"I can see you're busy. No problem. I really can't stay anyway. The kid's getting a little antsie here, which means I need to take her out and let her run. How would you like to go to lunch next Friday?"

I was so startled by the suggestion with Charles right there that I could feel myself tense up. The blood rushed to my head. Of course, Renata had no way of knowing who he was.

"I don't know," I said to her, then to Charles, "You guys coming over here or are we going over there next Friday? Are we even getting together next week?"

"I don't know," he said. He was still sitting in the client chair next to my desk. "You know how these women always work things out without telling us what the plans are. I'm sure my wife has the rest of our week planned for us already."

"Friday wouldn't be good for me, but another time might be fine."

"Okay, I'll call you," she said, standing up and chasing down her daughter who had squirmed off her lap again. She picked up the little girl and opened the front door. "'Bye."

"'Bye," I said.

She closed the door behind her. Charles stood up and came into the living room.

Got no Secrets to Conceal

"You ready to go?" he said, breaking the silence that had come over the place since the door closed.

"Yeah, sure, let's get outa' here," I replied, shifting uneasily on my feet.

Later that day she called and asked if she'd made anybody nervous earlier.

"No," I lied, for I knew how nervous I was when she'd asked me to lunch, "but we do have to get together and we will, another time."

"All right," she said.

About two months later, after returning from one of my walks on the Mall, there was a message from her on my answering device. She wanted to set up a time and day to go out to lunch, and would I call her back, let her know what was convenient for me? I dialed the number she left, and she picked up after two rings.

"Hello."

I instantly recognized her husky, Lauren Bacall sounding voice and my heart skipped a beat.

"Hi, Renata, this is Jack."

"Oh, hi, Jack. I'm so glad you called me back."

"So, yuh wan'a have lunch some time?" I was feeling really nervous. The question sounded dumb.

"I only need a couple day's notice so I can get a babysitter for Tess."

"How 'bout Friday. Debra and I aren't getting together with her folks this week. Wan'a do it then?"

"Yes. That sounds perfect. Want me to meet you at your office?"

"That'll be fine. Wha'da yuh say to twelve noon?"

15

"I'll be there," she said and broke the connection. It still hadn't sunk in that she might be interested in something other than just a lunch date, so I wrote her name down in my appointment book, not expecting anything or anticipating anything.

Two

When she arrived for the lunch date, she was dressed nicer than I'd ever seen her before. She'd suddenly been transformed from a frumpy looking housewife to a strictly business power executive. She was wearing tight black slacks that showed the perfect roundness of her voluptuous haunches. Her white blouse had ruffles in front, and that really focused my attention on her shapely breasts.

"Finally, we're getting together for lunch!" she said in that throaty purr she had. "I've been waiting a long time for this."

"Yes, indeed. Me too. It's been so long that I'm half tempted to just take you right now," I said, not thinking how daring the remark was.

"Take me," she said, flashing me a lascivious smile. Her flinty eyes sparked.

I thought she hesitated, as if she were waiting for me to lead her into my bedroom. I was only kidding when I made the comment. I still wasn't picking up on the signals she was putting down. Looking back on it now, I wonder at my naïveté. Those signals were so obvious.

After all this time and so much feinting and feigning, she was in my office and we were on our way to lunch. We went in her car to El Paisano, a burrito joint on Beach Street across from the carousel at the Boardwalk.

"You really do have a neat little home business," she said as we headed toward the beach. "I'm half tempted to tell Ramona about it, but I've decided I don't want to share any part of you with anybody else."

I didn't quite know how to take that. I guess I was finally picking up on the signals. I cooled it for now and made a noncommittal response.

"Who's Ramona?"

"The woman I work for."

"Yeah, well, I got it pretty good," I said, wondering exactly what "share any part of you" meant, "but it does have its disadvantages. I got'a make sure I get out'a the house every day, 'cause if I don't, I'll go stir."

"Oh, I know exactly what you're talking about. My guy wants to be a househusband. He has no idea. Thinks he'll be happy just staying home, but that's not all there is to tending to a kid. I think he'll see it differently after he's done it a while. He'll find out when I graduate and get a job."

"Doesn't sound like he knows what he's getting into," I said.

"It's what he says he wants," she shrugged. "He watched me go through housewife syndrome, so he kinda' knows what he's in for. I had it really bad right after Tess was born."

"You had what?"

"Housewife syndrome. If you're getting out of your house every day, you don't know what I'm talking about, so I'm not surprised you don't know what it is."

18

Got no Secrets to Conceal

"First I heard of it."

"It's what happens to women, mostly, after you have a baby, and you're stuck at home, and you don't have any adult contact all day."

"So that's what it's called. Exactly why I try to get outa' my place every day. I damn sure wouldn't wan'a hang around the house all day with a whining little kid. I'm not much of a kid person in the first place, and I don't think I'd make a good parent."

"Just your saying that tells me you'd be an excellent parent," she said. "At least it shows you have an awareness. That's more than can be said for most. You seemed pretty good with Tess that day I was in your office with her."

I thought the look on her face was one of tender admiration, a look that I would see again. We talked like that until we got to the res-taurant. We rolled over the railroad tracks and passed the Cocoanut Grove and Casino on the right. Because it was October, the beach and Boardwalk were quiet. Parking was no problem. She found a place across the street from the restaurant. We got our food to take out and walked over to the bleachers on the beach side of the Boardwalk.

As we ate our burritos, Renata turned the discussion to her sexual past, which turned out to be a promiscuous one. She started out by saying something about her "spouse" not worrying about whether she was "screwing" other guys, even though I suspected he probably did mind.

"I went out dancing with a friend once," she said. "It was the strangest thing. Here I was out on the

19

floor with a different guy for every number. When there's music playing and a place to dance, I can't help myself. I dance. My friend was turning down all these guys who were asking her to dance. She said she couldn't possibly dance with some other guy because she was married, and it just wouldn't be right. My *dancing* with other guys would be the least of Bill's worries, if he has any worries, which he doesn't seem to have. He just knows that if I want to get laid, I will, and that's all there is to it. Besides, he doesn't seem to have any interest in sex. I think he sees my promiscuity as an out for him."

I wondered what kind of a guy her husband must be, and why he'd want to be married to someone who'd cheat on him so indiscriminately. I'd never known any guy who'd knowingly be cuckolded, but then I didn't know this guy. Maybe if I ever met him, I'd see that she was right and that he really didn't care one way or the other.

"He knows what kind of a healthy sex drive I have; he must know that I'll satisfy it if I have to. Most of the time, I have to. Although, I'm surprised at how long I can go without it lately. Maybe it's because I'm secure in our relationship. One time I had sex with five guys in four nights. I think I could probably do it twice a day every day without batting an eye."

I nodded and didn't say a word. The thought of a possible sexual relationship with her was pushing its way into my consciousness. Why else would she be telling me all this if not eventually to be doing it with me? So, I thought I'd hang out for a while to see where it led.

20

Got no Secrets to Conceal

If the occasion arose, I'd just climb onto that sex drive of hers and go along for the ride, so to speak. For the briefest moment, I saw something (I couldn't say exactly what: a flash? a gleam?) appear fleetingly in her eyes as she gazed quizzically out at the waves breaking on the beach.

"You know, I've always thought it strange that I'm such a hot little number on one hand, and on the other, my astrological sign says I should be family oriented—and I am that too. I really do enjoy having a spouse and a kid, and I enjoy being with them around hearth and home, but I also like to get out and really party."

Like the barely perceived something that I'd seen in her eyes, so also I noticed something in her voice—a longing, a sadness. I couldn't pinpoint it, but it registered, and it would come back to haunt me. It would stir up a profound melancholy in me later. I saw the spark in her eyes, and I heard the longing in her voice, and I thought, *what the hell? After going together for seven years, Debra's and my sexual intimacy has become routine, almost boring. Renata's offering me something that seems so different, so exciting.*

We finished our lunch and sat gazing out at the surf. I picked up the food wrappers and empty beer bottles, put them in the bag and dropped it in a garbage can nearby. When I came back to where she was sitting, she suggested that we go for a walk along the beach. Once down on the sand, she took off her shoes. She was wearing nylons.

21

"Aren't you worried about getting sand in those stockings?" I asked.

"It's all right," she replied. "I'll take them off later. Let's just walk now."

As we strolled along the sand, she told me about how she and Bill were planning to eventually move out of California. They had misgivings about the California lifestyle, and they wanted to move someplace with a little slower pace. Arizona was a possibility. Her parents lived in Prescott.

"It would be nice to live closer to them, but not absolutely necessary," she said. "We really do like Sedona."

"I hear it's a beautiful place. Oak Creek Canyon."

"Have you been there?"

"Never have. Just heard a lot about it over the years."

"Yes, it is a beautiful place."

"'Magine it gets cold in the winter."

"I actually like to have four seasons."

"Not me. I been in Santa Cruz my whole life, and it gets cold enough for me in wintertime around here. Don't need any snow."

"Depends on what kind of jobs we can get, especially me. That'll trump everything including proximity to my parents."

When we got to the end of the beach at the river mouth, we turned and started back toward the Boardwalk.

Got no Secrets to Conceal

"So, wha'da yuh think?" I blurted out, not really knowing how else to do it. "Wan'a get laid?"

"Be all right with me." She responded quickly just like she'd done back at the office. "We could have another lunch date and skip the lunch."

So it was that easy. We were going to be lovers, barring some unforeseen circumstance. We continued our stroll back to the restaurant. We got a couple more beers and went over to a table. She went to the restroom as I sat down and thought about our first tryst. I wondered if I could satisfy her as I thought about her professed active sex life. How could any one person gratify such a voracious sexual appetite? I wouldn't worry about that until the time came. And really, why worry about it at all? She came out of the restroom and sat down across the table from me.

"Where we go'n'a make love?" I asked.

"I don't know," she replied. We'll have to figure something out."

"We could go back to my place right now. It's nice and comfortable, and I won't be seeing Debra until later this afternoon. I do have an appointment at three, so that gives us a little over an hour."

"I don't think so. I really don't want our first time to be a quickie. I've been waiting too long for this, and I want to have some time with you. You know it's been almost eighteen months that I've been waiting."

"Really?" I said, raising an eyebrow in surprise. "I wouldn't have thought so."

Just the thought of it got me hard. We drank our beers and talked small talk, both barely able to contain

23

our excitement. The rest of our lunch date was thus consumed. She told me she had to pick up Tess at the babysitter. She offered to take me back to my place, but I told her I needed to go to the savings and loan first and asked her if she would drop me off there. She said she would and we were off. When we got to the savings and loan at Soquel and Front, I told her to pull into the parking lot behind the place. She pulled into a space and shut the motor off. Then she turned and faced me, her slender arm extended across her knee which was lifted slightly onto the seat so that her torso wouldn't be twisted. I reached my hand across to the back of her neck and drew her to me. As I kissed her, I slid my other hand up her flank to her breast. She fell forward into my arms, so I relaxed and enjoyed this moment for as long as I could. When we stopped kissing, she whispered in my ear,

"It's about time. I was beginning to wonder when and if you were ever going to do that."

She held my head between her palms and kissed me passionately.

As I walked back to my place, I ran into Jean Kaiser on the Mall. I couldn't miss her. At five-eleven she's about an inch taller than I, and she is beautiful with dark hair and blue eyes, like Debra. Jean was a friend of mine from high school. She was my senior year prom date. She'd gone to Cabrillo right after graduation and gotten her A.J. certificate after two years in the program. She did all that while I was at San Jose State. By the time I got my checker job, she'd already worked her way up from a clerical job at the police department to being the police spokeswoman. She's the one who was quoted

24

Got no Secrets to Conceal

in the newspaper when a crime made the headlines. We were longtime friends, and even though we flirted a lot, there never was any real romance between us. She loved Debra and was happy for both of us that we had such a good relationship. Jean herself had a couple of relationships over the years, but never married or even got engaged.

"Hey, how're yuh doing, handsome?" she said as we got closer.

"Okay. How 'bout yourself?"

"Great. Where yuh goin'?"

"Headin' back to the house. Just had a lunch date with a client," I lied, suddenly feeling guilty for the lie and the lunch date itself.

"I'll walk with you. I'm going back to the department."

At the time the police department was in one wing of the city hall which was a couple blocks north of my bungalow on Center Street. A few years later, a new facility would be built about three blocks south of it.

"So, yuh wan'a go to lunch a day next week?" I said.

"Sure. Gi'me a call soon as yuh get back to your office and we'll set something up."

"Okay."

We split up at Walnut and Center and went to our respective offices. I called her right away, and we had a lunch date on Tuesday.

Three

Renata called me first thing Monday morning just to say hello and to chat. In the meantime, I'd called a couple of the motels down on Beach Street to see what their rates were. I didn't really want to meet her at my place, because Debra had a key and could show up anytime. Hers was out of the question. We really did need a neutral spot that neither her spouse nor Debra knew about. At least that's the way I felt about it. She was much more open. I told her about the motels, and she agreed that would be best.

Hearing from her made me feel so good. I got light-hearted at the sound of her voice, especially considering the subject we were discussing. I was experiencing the first buzz of infatuation. I wondered if she was having similar feelings. I thought I sensed titillation, an excitement in her voice. I felt a quaver in my own as I spoke.

"The cost of a room seems to be standard, right around twenty-five bucks."

"Twelve-fifty each isn't so bad. I think I can afford that," she said.

"When do you wan'a get together? I'm free most days. Free until four o'clock, that is. That's usually the time Debra gets home from school. Sometimes she calls me and wants us to do something together."

Got no Secrets to Conceal

"I understand," she said. "Now all we have to do is figure out a convenient day and time. Any day except Tuesday or Thursday. I've got classes those days."

"Okay."

"Probably Monday would be best, 'cause I can usually get a sitter on that day. One of the ladies in the neighborhood whose little girl is Tess's age."

"'Sounds good to me. Just tell me the Monday."

"It'll be soon. Count on it. In fact, I don't know if I can wait much longer. I've waited too long already."

And with that, she made a husky, throaty sound, and that stirred my desire for her.

"So, what're yuh doin' today? Yuh got a sitter?" I asked.

"Yes, and I'm going up to campus to talk to my counselor. Hopefully he'll tell me I can graduate in June. I think I only need three more classes. If that's it, I'll take two in winter quarter and one in the spring. I'm taking two this quarter. I'll be glad when it's over. I'm tired of going to school. I'm ready to get out. Get a job. Make some money."

"It *is* nice to be making your own money, for sure. I know Debra's always had a great attitude, and I'm sure it's because she makes good money. She's got the best self-esteem of any woman I've ever known."

"Just wait till you guys get married and start having kids. That'll change things. It's demeaning to do a job and not get paid for it. Besides housewifery, the only other kind I can think of is slavery. Although, none of what I just said really applies to me. I handle all the money for our household. I'm good at it and Bill isn't. I

27

deposit his paycheck and give him a hundred dollars. He gets paid every two weeks, so the hundred dollars is supposed last that long. He likes not having all the responsibility of taking care of our finances. Speaking of which, I've got some things to do around here before I go up to the university, so I'd better hang up and get to them. I'll be calling you soon and we'll get that motel room."

It was a warm Indian summer morning, so I decided to take a walk to the end of the wharf. It would've been nice to meet her that day, but she couldn't, and I'd just have to live with it. I walked the straight-line down Center Street to Washington Street where it bends left and goes to the wharf. The late morning sun was brilliant, shimmering off the blue surface of Monterey Bay. As I approached the wharf, I saw the P.G.&E. plant at Moss Landing, something white billowing from its stacks.

I began thinking how after I'd first met Renata, I'd be out on one of my walks thinking about sex and how nice it would be to be getting some, not even thinking that I'd ever be getting it from her. I'd walk past some anonymous house and imagine that a woman would open the front door and seductively beckon me. But then I'd snap back to reality, suddenly realizing that that sort of thing only happened in the movies or to someone else. Then I imagined that some beautiful woman would pick me out right then on the wharf, or I would see one in distress, ready to jump and I'd save her, but then again I knew that was only fiction, the stuff that plays like *Anna Kleiber* were made of. The reality

28

Got no Secrets to Conceal

was that a lot of disheveled people (men and women) lined the railings, their fishing lines in the water, seagull and pigeon shit everywhere. Not a very romantic picture to be sure.

I walked all the way out to the end of the wharf, turned and started back, my enthusiasm to sit down and enjoy the sun and sea dampened by the smattering of bird droppings. I made my way back to the beach. As little as I had to do and as boring as the day was turning out, I thought I should be thankful I could relax, for tomorrow might not be this hassle-free. I had two insurance cases I was working on, and from day to day, I'd either be busy on both or nothing was happening.

I walked out West Cliff to the point. This was Steamer Lane, one of the best point breaks in the state. Locals referred to it as the Lane. I watched the surfers for a while, and then the wind started kicking up on the cliff and out on the water. Spindrift swept into the surfers' faces as they were getting up to ride down the face of a five- or six-footer.

I couldn't get Renata out of my head. I wanted to see if I could find her on campus. Maybe take her out to lunch.

I got up there by one o'clock. I didn't have a clue where to find her, so I went to the Bay Tree Bookstore and looked around. Not much going on there. I went next door to the coffee shop, and there she was standing in line. I walked up behind her and tapped her on the shoulder.

"I was hoping I'd run into you," I said.

29

"Well, hello," she said with a pleasant smile. "What are you doing here?"

"I came looking for you."

"Oh, how sweet. Well, you've found me. Now what?"

"How 'bout I buy yuh lunch?"

"You're just so sweet all around today. I'd love to have lunch with you."

We sat and talked over lunch for about an hour. We acted like a couple teenagers in love, even though I was pushing forty and she was ten years younger. Still, we were well past adolescence, and should've been acting more like the adults we both were.

So ended our second lunch date, which was only a chance meeting. Really, what were the odds I'd run into her on such a whim. She offered to drive me back to my place. I accepted, and when we got there, there were no parking places on the street, so she drove three doors up to the public parking lot and found a place on the end where her windshield was facing north on Center Street.

"I really can't stay. Tess has been with the sitter for three hours."

"I understand completely."

When I leaned over to kiss her, she gently took hold of the back of my neck and firmly pulled me to her, giving me the sexiest French kiss I'd ever had up till then. I responded by fondling her ample breast and moving my hand down her flank to her supple haunch. As quickly as it started, it ended. When I turned around in the seat to get out, I saw a police car coming down Center Street. I got out and looked straight at Jean who was

30

Got no Secrets to Conceal

riding along in the police cruiser. She had a knowing look on her face. I could feel the blood rush to my head.

"I really must go," Renata said in a playful tone.

I hoped my uneasiness didn't show. I didn't say anything to Renata to let her know how self-conscious I felt after I saw Jean. Ambivalent feelings overcame me as I watched her drive away. On the one hand I felt so good about the infatuation developing between us, and on the other I just got busted by Jean and was going to have some explaining to do tomorrow at lunch.

Four

I met Jean on Tuesday at Jack's on the corner of Cedar and Lincoln. We had hamburgers and cokes, like we used to do back in high school at Anne's on Beach Street. Jean didn't waste any time getting to the point.

"So, who was the girl I saw you with yesterday? Didn't look like Debra."

"'Cause it wasn't Debra."

"Yeah? Then who was it?"

"A client," I lied.

"Same client you had lunch with last week when I saw you?"

"No, different one," I lied again. "One the other day was a guy thinks his wife's having an affair. Wants me to find out if it's true."

"Oh. What else is new?" Thankfully that was the end of her probing about Renata.

"Not much. Startin' to get busy."

Yet another lie. I still only had the two insurance jobs and the pro bono job I was doing for Charles Morrison.

"How 'bout you, girl? Gettin' any lately?"

Jean and I had known each other for such a long time that we could talk to each other like that, and neither of us would be offended. Most of the time it was just innocent flirting.

Got no Secrets to Conceal

"Had a date on Saturday. Seemed like a nice enough guy, but I don't know. At least he didn't seem intimidated by my job."

"Where'd yuh go?"

"New Riverside for dinner. Warmth was playing, so we danced some after. Had a good time."

"Sounds like fun."

We were quiet for a couple minutes. Jean broke the silence.

"How're your folks? Talk to them lately?"

"Yeah, last week. They like Morro Bay a lot. Foggier there than here. Dad's enjoying retirement. Still playing golf couple times a week. Mom's gotten into a bridge group. They're both still buggin' me to marry Debra."

"Yeah, I'll second that."

"Oh, please."

"Isn't it about time you made her an honest woman."

"I've still got'a get busier in the office. Don't wan'a be a drag on her income."

"Pretty lame, if yuh ask me. And that reminds me. I know someone who might need your help. My friend Kendra was dating a guy for a couple months and she broke it off with him, but he keeps pestering her."

"She get a restraining order against him?"

"Well, no. She doesn't think it's that serious yet. I gave her your number, and she's probably go'n'a call you soon?"

"Okay. I *am* getting busier, but I'm still takin' on new cases. I look forward to hearing from her."

33

We finished our lunches. Jean went back to the police station and I went back to my office. I checked my phone messages, and sure enough, there was one from Jean's friend Kendra. I called her back and she picked up after the second ring.

"What can I do for you?" I asked after I introduced myself.

"Have you spoken to Jean?"

"I just had lunch with her, and she told me some guy's bothering you?"

"Yes, he keeps calling me, and I keep telling him I don't want to see him anymore."

"Why don't you get a restraining order?"

"Jean tells me it'll cost a hundred and fifty dollars. I really can't afford that right now, and I don't think he's that serious a threat. I think all he needs is a good talking to by someone in authority."

"And you think I'm a serious enough authority?"

"Well, yeah. You'll see what I mean when you meet him."

"First, I think you should know that I charge a hundred dollars a day plus expenses. From the sound of it, I probably won't put in more'n a couple hours, and I can't see that there are go'n'a be any expenses, so if that's what it ends up being, then I'll only charge you for half a day. That's about a third the amount you'd pay to get the restraining order."

"Boy, you're just as nice as Jean told me you'd be. That sounds like a good deal. Thanks."

Got no Secrets to Conceal

"Can you come to my office and we can sign a contract, and you can tell me more about this unwanted suitor?"

"When would you like me to be there? I can come right now."

"Great. I'll see yuh in a bit."

I gave her my address, and she was there within ten minutes. She was an attractive, tall blond with blue eyes. We signed one of my standard contracts, and she gave me a hundred dollars cash. Then we talked. I filled out a three by five card with her name, Kendra Moon, phone number and address. She lived in a bungalow court on Walnut Avenue down the hill from Santa Cruz High. I got my notebook out and started taking notes.

"Okay. Now, what's this guy's name?" I asked.

"Ryan Sullivan. He's really a nice guy; he just won't take no for an answer."

"You have an address and phone number on 'im? Where's he work?"

I wrote down the information she gave me. He worked at Sylvania over in Harvey West Park.

"So, what exactly is he doing to annoy you?"

"For one thing, he calls me on the telephone every day. I quit answering, but then he leaves a message. He tells me how much he loves me, and he wants to see me again. Sometimes he stops by my house without calling me first. I don't invite him in, and he usually leaves, but sometimes he hangs around by my front door. I just want him to leave me alone."

"Okay, here's what I'm go'n'a do. First, I'll go over to Sylvania, catch him off guard on the job. I'll

35

have a little chat with him. Convince him that it's in his best interest to leave you alone."

"I don't want you to hurt him."

"Don't worry about that. This is only go'n'a be the first visit. We'll see how he responds to that before we consider taking another tack. If what you've told me about him is accurate, I'm guessing I won't even have to pay him a second visit."

She left and I got ready to go have a talk with Mr. Sullivan. I went straight up Center Street to Mission and cut across the park in front of Holy Cross church. Then I crossed over the freeway on the footbridge. From there I went down the bike path into Harvey West. The receptionist in the front office at Sylvania was an attractive brunette. The name plate on her desk identified her as Pamela Hurd.

"Hello, Pamela. I'd like to speak to Ryan Sullivan," I said as I showed her my P.I. ticket. I wanted his employer to know that a private investigator was inquiring after him. She looked at it closely and said,

"May I inquire what this is about?"

"You may, but then I'd have to tell you it's a confidential matter."

"Very well. He just got back from his lunch break. I'll see if he's back at his desk."

She offered me a seat by the door, and then she punched in a couple numbers on her phone. She spoke so softly that I really couldn't make out what she said to him. She disconnected the call and said,

"He'll be right out, Mr. Lefevre."

"Thanks."

Got no Secrets to Conceal

Not a minute later this fairly good-looking guy stepped out of a door behind the receptionist's desk. He wore a tie, but the cuffs of his white shirt were rolled up. I was sort of half-expecting a nerdy looking guy. I think I got that impression when Kendra said she didn't want me to hurt him. He looked like your average preppy. Probably a frat. boy in college. Now a junior exec. The receptionist gave him my card, pointed me out to him, and he came over, his right hand extended. I stood up and shook his hand.

"Would you like to step outside?" I said. "What I have to say to you is rather confidential."

"Oh, really? That why you came in here flashing your badge?"

"I don't have a badge, sir. Don't mistake me for the police."

"Very well then. Let's go outside."

His second response was more subdued than the first. I think he realized the receptionist was listening to our exchange. Once outside, we walked over to the parking lot where nobody was around to eaves drop on our conversation.

"I'm representing Kendra Moon. She says you're being a nuisance. Only reason she doesn't have a restraining order out on you is because she was talked out of it by a friend. You need to quit bothering her. Do you understand?"

He was looking a bit sheepish. Kendra was right. All he needed was someone to talk to him, dissuade him, and judging from the way he looked, I succeeded in doing it.

"I want you to say you understand. Do you?"

"Yes! I understand."

"If I have to come back and talk to you again, it's not go'n'a go as easy as it did today."

"You don't have to threaten me."

"Hey, I don't threaten. I'm just giving you some friendly advice. I wonder how your employer would take it if he knew you were out stalking young women."

"Okay, okay! I get it!"

The fear rising in his voice was palpable.

"All right, then. Just leave Kendra alone."

And with that, I turned and walked back to the bike path and headed home. When I got back to the house, there was a message on my answering machine from Renata. Boy, it was sure nice to hear her voice after dealing with that creep. I called her back and we talked briefly. Then I called Kendra and told her about the meeting. I told her to call me if he bothered her anymore, and if he didn't, I'd refund fifty dollars to her the following Monday. She didn't call me, so I called her on Monday and went over to her place and gave her the money.

"Now be sure to call me if he bothers you again." I said.

"Don't worry. I will."

Five

I didn't talk to Renata again for another eight days. It was Wednesday morning at about ten o'clock, two days after I refunded Kendra's money. She said she'd be in town that day, and would I like to meet her someplace for lunch? I didn't have anything going on, so I told her I'd meet her at Zoccolli's delicatessen at the north end of the Mall. I had some work to do on one of the insurance claims I was investigating. It was the same case I'd been working on the week before. I hadn't been anxious to work on it lately, but now that I knew I was going to be seeing Renata in a couple hours, I got right back into it. I was hoping we'd be able to get off alone, do some snuggling and kissing. I started thinking about different ways I could get to that point.

At ten to twelve I locked my door and started off to the Mall. As I approached the delicatessen, I saw her sitting on the planter box out in front. There were already quite a few people eating their lunches around her.

"Hi," she said as I approached.

"Hi. how are yuh? Long time no see."

"Indeed. It must be all of a week, maybe eight days. Next time'll be even longer, but not by much. In fact, if you're available, it'll be Monday after next. I think we ought to get that motel room then."

"Sounds good to me," I replied as we entered the delicatessen.

There were a lot of people scrambling for their lunches. When we finally placed our orders, I got a hot pastrami, and Renata ordered a turkey sandwich. We walked over to San Lorenzo Park to eat next to the duck pond and enjoy the afternoon sun. Renata lost no time getting to the point.

"So, what time do you want to meet on Monday?" she asked.

"Oh, I don't know. Who's go'n'a get the room you 'r me?"

"I can do that. Put it on my credit card."

"Aren't yuh worried about Bill seeing it?"

"No. He never checks stuff like that. Like I said, I take care of the household finances. I deposit his paycheck and give him cash when he needs it."

"What time can yuh check in?"

"I don't know. I'm guessing the earliest would probably be one o'clock. I'll check when I make the reservation."

"The next question is where? I kinda' like the Casa Blanca. I been by there a few times on my bike, and it looks like the coolest one."

"That sounds fine."

"Good. So, here's what we'll do. You go ahead and get the room and call me. Let me know the room number, and I'll just come right over. You shouldn't have any trouble finding a phone nearby. There's a pay phone right at the entrance to the motel on Beach Street."

40

Got no Secrets to Conceal

"I don't believe this," she said a bit ironically. "This is the first time I've gotten the room key. I like it. I feel empowered."

"Hey, I'll let you be the driver."

"Most guys would insist on getting the key themselves, and let me tell you, I've had a lot of experience."

"Well it just works out better for me that way. I know too many people in this town, and I really don't want to be seen getting a motel room in the middle of the day, whereas you, being from Boulder Creek, probably don't know that many people down here."

"I really don't care if I'm seen or not," she said.

We finished our sandwiches and were watching the ducks. A woman was giving her two children breadcrumbs and they were scattering them as the ducks scurried about trying to get them. One of the ducks dominated the action, scooping up a bread crumb, then moving on taking other crumbs away from the other ducks. His appetite seemed insatiable, and he seemed to be at the top of the pecking order.

"Aggressive little bugger, isn't he?" I said as we watched the competition.

"Reminds me of some of the guys I've known," she replied. "I've got to be going now. I'll get Tess from the babysitter, and we'll meet Donna and Hazel and go look for something for Tess's birthday. She's going to be two next month. We're going to have a little party for her, and I still haven't gotten her anything, not that it'll make much difference since her grandparents have al-

ready sent a big box, which I imagine is filled with presents. Grandparents tend to indulge their grandchildren."

"I guess! Debra's parents are pressuring us to
get married, so they'll have grandchildren to indulge."

We left the park and walked toward the Mall on
Cooper Street. She'd parked in the double deck parking
structure one block on the other side of the Mall.

"A guy I used to date called me yesterday," she
said. "First I've heard from him in two years."

As she talked, she got a dreamy look on her
face, a look that I'd seen before, a look that also seemed
to have a shade of sadness.

"I had the biggest crush on this guy, and I didn't
tell him for the longest time. I was really taken with him.
When I finally did tell him how I felt about him, he said
it was a good thing I hadn't told him earlier, because if I
had, he said he would've ended it right then. So now he
calls me again. I wonder why?"

When she said this, her face was consumed with
that secret expression that she affected so well.

"And of course, now you're not interested,
right?" I said, assuming the obvious.

"Well, I wouldn't exactly say that," she said, but
she didn't elaborate.

As we approached the Cooper House, we could
hear the band playing on the patio. We crossed the street,
and as we passed the music, Renata said,

"Good thing we're on this side of the street. I'm
such a dancing fool that I'd probably start dancing if we
were right next to the music. That's one of the things I
do that drives Bill crazy."

Got no Secrets to Conceal

"What does he do when he's with you and you do somethin' like that?" I asked.

"He walks away from me and acts like he doesn't know me."

When we got to her car, I hugged her and kissed her passionately. She responded in kind.

I walked back to my office stepping lightly with the anticipation of my upcoming rendezvous with Renata at the Casa Blanca Inn. I now had little interest in some woman opening her door and beckoning me into her inner sanctum. I was flooded with thoughts of meeting Renata the following Monday and making hot love to her. Knowing this made the rest of my week go by quickly, but because of my anticipation and desire to be with her, time seemed to crawl at a snail's pace. I was struck by the ambivalence of these opposing sensations. Confusion set in as I was feeling the speed and inertia all at once in undulating sequences. I'd sit in my office working on a case, and my mind would wander from the task at hand. I'd try to analyze this new situation, but it did me little good, so I tried to put it out of my mind. I couldn't stop thinking about her, and it got worse after we became lovers. Hence, I spent the ten days until the next time I saw her confused and distracted. During that time and after when I was with Debra, I found myself hearing her, but not listening to her. She'd say things to me and ask me questions, and I'd ask her to repeat herself, and then I wouldn't really hear her when she did. I seemed to be constantly preoccupied with Renata.

The big day finally came and all my anxiety and anticipation suddenly seemed anti-climactic. After I finished shaving and showering, I took a walk along the Mall. I had another couple hours before Renata would call and tell me the room number at the Casa Blanca. Indian summer was coming to an end, and there was a slight coolness in the air. The sky was blue, and the air crystal clear. I was feeling just fine. On Pacific Avenue shop owners were opening their doors and sweeping their sidewalks, getting ready for the business day. The clock tower chimed eleven o'clock. In a couple more hours, I'd be with Renata in a motel room. The thought of it excited me once again.

On the trip back to the office, I walked through Logos, my favorite bookstore in town. Used books went for half the cover price, and there was always good jazz playing on the sound system. Even if I didn't get a book, I still enjoyed listening to the music. A John Coltrane record, *Giant Steps*, was playing as I looked through the paperback fiction section. I bought a copy of Judith Rossner's *To the Precipice*. I didn't know what it was about, but I'd read *Looking for Mr. Goodbar* and liked it, so I decided if this one was that good, it would be worth the dollar price tag. After I got home, I sat down and started to read the book while I waited for Renata's call.

"Hi," she said at quarter after one when I answered the phone.

"Hi," I said. "What's up?"

"Well, it's room twenty-four. Wait'll you see it. It's really nice. There's a great view."

"Okay. I'll be there in about ten minutes. See yuh then."

44

Got no Secrets to Conceal

"Get here quickly. I can't wait much longer," she replied, and hung up.

I set out immediately, locking my door as I left. When I got to the motel, I went up the steps and the room was right there on the first landing. I knocked and she let me in.

"Well, wha'da yuh think?" she asked, opening her arms, taking in the entire room. "Nice, huh?"

"God, I guess," I replied.

She drew back the curtains, and we took in the expansive view of Monterey Bay with the Municipal Wharf right in front of us. We stood dreamy eyed for a few minutes viewing the peaceful scene before us, and I suddenly became conscious of being seen by someone I might know who would in turn tell Debra that I was in a motel room in the middle of the day with some strange woman, so I stepped aside momentarily before realizing how absurd the idea was. Thinking about it, I could see that the possibility was remote, so I relaxed, but not before she noticed how I'd tensed up. She made no comment about my uneasiness. She closed the curtains and directed me into the bathroom where I found a bottle of Christian Brothers chardonnay on ice in the wash basin.

"I brought a corkscrew, too. Open it and pour some for us." she said. "I thought it'd be nice to have something to drink."

"Good thinking," I replied. "Nothing like a little wine to make us mellow. Oh, by the way, how much was the room. I owe yuh some money."

"It came to twenty-six-fifty with tax," she said.

I took fifteen dollars out of my billfold and set it down next to her purse. It felt like I was dealing with a prostitute, even though I wasn't giving her the money for any services rendered. It was ridiculous for me to think that way because fifteen dollars would've been a cheap trick.

"Did you pay in cash?" I asked, not knowing why.

"I paid with plastic," she said.

"You don't care what Bill's go'n'a say when he sees that credit card bill?"

"I told you he'll never see it. I handle all the money and bills in our house."

"Oh, that's right. You told me that."

She got the wine from the bathroom basin and handed it to me along with the corkscrew. Then she unwrapped the two plastic glasses that were in the room, and I poured some wine into both. She held hers up and proposed a toast to a long and loving friendship. Then we embraced and kissed. As we separated, she moved to one side of the bed, and, turning down the covers, she said, "don't peak, now," and started to undress. I took my clothes off too, and within seconds we were in the bed making feverish love, the likes of which I'd never experienced in my life. When the initial burst was over and we both lay spent on the bed, I pondered how special Renata was, and my desire for her was now intensifying so much that I didn't think it could get much stronger. I would see later that this was just the beginning.

Got no Secrets to Conceal

"Why are you so tense?" she asked as I lay on top of her.

She was lightly massaging my neck and shoulders. I was feeling quite relaxed and didn't really know what she meant. I looked to one side. I was confused by the question.

"Wha'da yuh mean? I feel very relaxed."

"You just feel tense to me right in here," she said, touching the area just below the nape.

"Sometimes I get stress pains around there. Must be the spot where my tension all comes together. Only thing I can think of."

Then I rolled off her and was lying on my back next to her staring at the ceiling. I snuck a sidelong glance in her direction, and she had that faraway, quizzical look in her eyes again, the corners of her mouth curling up into a slight smile. This time I didn't let it go by without comment.

"What?" I asked.

"Oh, I was just thinking how long it's been since I've done something like this. Must be two years since I got a motel room with someone. For me that's a long time, and I never got the key myself."

I tried not to let it show, but it pained me to hear this kind of comment. The ambivalence was kicking in again, producing the opposite effect. The remark stirred my lustful instincts. She made me feel like I was a john, and she was my hooker date. I began making wild love to her again. I was consumed with her and couldn't stop touching her.

47

After our second session, she read to me from a book of poems written by Dylan Thomas. We made love two more times. After the third time she said,

"Whew, you really know how to show a woman a good time, don't you? Can't remember screwing like that in a long time. I remember one time screwing for what seemed like hours, and sure enough, it was—hours, that is. 'What time is it, anyway?' I said to the guy, looking at my watch, 'one o'clock; that makes six hours.' Can you believe it? Six hours! That's what this reminds me of."

I had mixed feelings about what she was telling me. Ambivalence yet again. On one hand, it was a real ego booster since it made me feel especially sexually adept; at least that seemed to be her view of me. On the other hand, hearing about her previous sexual exploits bothered me. I didn't want to hear it. When I tried for a fifth time at four o'clock, she said,

"Do we really have time for this?"

"Wouldn't you like to do it again?" I asked.

"I wouldn't mind, but I really don't think we have time," she said, picking up her watch from the nightstand and looking at it. "I really do have to pick Tess up from the sitter."

"Yeah. I guess you're right. I should be scooting outa' here myself."

I got up out of the bed and went in to take a shower. I was feeling wonderful. No woman had ever given me that much or such good sex in my life. Now all I wanted to know was when would be the next time. When I came out of the shower, she was still in bed

48

Got no Secrets to Conceal

reading from another book she'd brought along, probably from one of her classes. I leaned down and kissed her goodbye and told her I'd be thinking about her. She said she'd do the same, and then I was out the door.

As I walked along Beach Street, I decided to go up to Dutra Overlook on West Cliff Drive. There was a great view of Cowell's Beach, the Wharf and Boardwalk, and the Monterey Bay coastline. With my forearms resting on the fence railing, I took a moment to contemplate what had just happened. From that vantage point, I could see the Casa Blanca Inn, and as I stood there, I saw the door to room twenty-four open and Renata come out, but I couldn't make her out clearly; I only knew because I was looking directly at the room we'd been in and who else could it be? I watched her disappear around the corner and out the side, and at that moment I had an intense feeling of happy melancholy. I wasn't in love with her yet, but I was experiencing a profound sense of tenderness toward her. I also knew that this was no ordinary woman, and I had a feeling that this wasn't going to be just another affair. With these thoughts tumbling through my head, I started down the hill.

Six

The inevitable comparisons between Debra and Renata came to mind, but I tried to put them out of it since there were really no comparisons at all, only contrasts. Debra was sweet and innocent with the schoolteacher's resolve, one of the most common-sense people I'd ever known. She had a great personality and a sense of humor. Renata, on the other hand, was strictly business, sensuous, kind of like a cat, snuggling up against you on the couch in one moment and baring claws the next.

It was time, maybe past time, to start thinking with the head on my shoulders rather the other one. But was I going to do that? Probably not. All I could think of at that moment was Renata, and that's all I wanted to do until the next time I talked to her. That wouldn't be for another two weeks. I probably should have called her sooner, but after a week of not hearing from her, I started to get feelings of insecurity. She didn't seem as eager as I was. I started to think that she was having second thoughts about seeing me again, but when she finally did call on Tuesday two weeks later, she told me nothing was further from the truth.

"I thought I'd heard the last of you," I said, trying to sound disinterested.

I started to build up my defenses by telling myself I wasn't going to let her know I was hurting, wasn't

Got no Secrets to Conceal

going to let her know how much I thought of her and cared for her.

"What gave you that idea?" she replied.

"It was just that I hadn't heard from you in so long. That's all."

"I've been really busy and didn't want to call you and just talk for a few minutes, but that's the way it turned out, anyway. I really can't talk long right now. I was just on my way up to campus, and I've got to drop my kid off at the babysitter on the way, but I did want to get back to you to let you know that I'm thinking about you, and I'll be calling soon. We've got to have lunch again. We need to talk about the next time we can get together for. I've got to go now, so take care and I'll be in touch soon."

"Okay. Talk to you later. Thanks for calling."

This conversation made me feel better, but I was still apprehensive. I wouldn't feel completely reassured until she was in my arms and we were making love once again, but even then, I wasn't sure I'd feel completely certain about her. In fact, I didn't know if I'd ever be sure of her, but I was glad she'd called me back, and I was looking forward to hearing from her and seeing her again.

I was beginning to realize that I shouldn't get too attached to her. After all she was married, had a kid, and was planning on moving away. I knew from the start that at some point I'd have to let her go and never see her again. These thoughts were driving me to distraction. I was having difficulty concentrating on the

51

work I was doing, and this wasn't the best time in my new career to be having any anxiety in my personal life.

I got busy on the job hoping it would take my mind off the uncertainties of the relationship. It had been a month since I'd spoken to Kendra. I called her to follow up on her case. She hadn't heard from Sullivan since when I told him to leave her alone. Case closed.

The insurance job was a simple liability case. A guy who was riding in a car that was involved in a small traffic accident claimed he was suffering from whiplash. He was asking more than the insurance company was offering. I was doing some surveillance on him to see if he was faking it. I mostly organized my notes, called the company and brought my contact there up to speed.

By the end of the day, I was feeling good from having gotten over my distraction and putting in a full day's work. I was feeling so good, in fact, that I tried to snuggle with Debra after we got in bed. She was spending the night with me. We did that at least one night a week. She'd either come to my place, or I'd go to hers. That night she didn't want to make love, and her response to my advances ended by her pushing me away. It was so disheartening that it almost spoiled the sensation of the whole rest of the day, but I rolled over and turned my back to her, wondering what it would take to be her lover again.

The more I thought about it, the less interested I was in that aspect of my relationship with Debra. I tried to remember the last time we had sexual relations, but I couldn't, so my thoughts reverted to Renata, and just as soon as her image appeared in my consciousness, I felt a

Got no Secrets to Conceal

profound sense of contentment, and I drifted off into gentle sleep with that pleasant image planted in my brain.

I picked up another insurance claim case, so I stayed quite busy over the next few days, which helped me to deal with Renata's absence. She remained constantly in my thoughts, but I was too busy to long for or miss her much. It seemed that everything was happening at once. As autumn waned and winter approached, a chill came into the air and remained even when the sun was at its brightest.

She called on Monday after Thanksgiving to arrange a meeting with me the following Monday at the Terrace Court motel, which was next door to the Casa Blanca. She said she wanted to book a different motel because she didn't want to get a "reputation." Her use of the word puzzled me because it seemed to contradict her earlier statements about not caring who saw her no matter what the circumstances. For my part, I'd always been very cautious when I was with Renata, sometimes looking furtively around me to see if I saw anybody I knew, but I never did, and even if friends or acquaintances were around, they'd probably be too engrossed in their own thoughts to even notice us. The bottom line was that not many people ever really noticed much outside of their own sphere.

When she set the following Monday to meet again, it was all I could do to control my excitement. At last it was going to happen. We were going to be lovers again. I wondered if she was feeling a similar intensity. I needed something for a distraction, but I was begin-ning to see that there would be nothing that would take my mind off the situation. My thoughts went back and forth between good feelings about her and bad, and the ambivalence was obvious.

She called again on Friday morning to make sure everything was set for Monday. She told me she'd get the room at one o'clock again and that she'd call like she did the last time to let me know the room number. So, everything was set. I went surfing on Saturday, and on Sunday Debra and I went to San José to visit Charles and Frances.

I was completely distracted in San José. I stayed pretty much to myself, taking short walks around the neighborhood and reading the Sunday newspaper or the Rossner novel in the living room while Debra hung around with Charles and Frances in the family room with the television on in the background. Frances was an avid football fan. She watched N.F.L. games on Sundays during the season. Charles wasn't crazy about television (he was kind of grumpy in general, and there wasn't much he did like), so he fooled around with the Sunday crossword, sipped on his Chivas Regal, and complained about the distraction of the television. I was always the odd man out when I was at Charles' and Frances' house. They seemed to tolerate me, the price they paid to spend time with their daughter. I was outside on the patio, and I saw a large red rock next to a planter.

"Where'd you get that?" I asked as Charles came out to join me.

"That came from Oak Creek Canyon, Sedona, Arizona," he replied. "Frances and I were traveling through there, what was it, maybe five years ago. All the soil up in there is red like that. Everywhere you look, red soil and rocks. I just couldn't help stopping and picking up that one."

Renata's image jumped out at me in my mind's eye. Sedona was one of the places she said she and her spouse were looking at to move to.

"Pretty country up there, is it?" I asked. "I've never been."

"Beautiful country," Charles responded. "Only other place I've ever seen red soil like that was over on the island of Kauai, but Oak Creek Canyon's a little more to my liking. Kauai's too much jungle; Sedona's more of a desert climate. I like it better. Didn't like the humidity in Kauai. Too tropical for me."

"I suppose Debra and I ought'a get down to Arizona, have a look. 'Sounds like a pretty place. I've only been through Arizona on Route 66 a couple times. I never really stopped and looked around."

"Actually, if you were on Route 66, you went right by Oak Creek Canyon, only a few miles south of the highway."

As we talked, we moved around the patio. He bent down occasionally and picked out a leaf here, a twig there, keeping his garden neatly manicured. There were planters at ground level around the perimeter of the patio. They were about two feet wide on three sides. All of it was bordered by a six-foot-high concrete block wall. Charles usually put in a vegetable garden year-round. Now, in early December, he had five rows of vegetables on three sides of his patio: peas, carrots,

55

beets, spinach, and lettuce. He pointed each one out as we made the rounds. He'd harvested the summer garden in late September and planted this one a month later.

Charles was such a perfectionist that it some-times made me feel incompetent, but then that was part and parcel of our relationship. After Debra and I had been going out for about a year and had a strong rela-tionship, she'd gone to her father's house, as she always did, to have him change the oil in her car. He'd remarked sarcastically that she should get her boyfriend to do the job for her. It had been a case of the father losing his little girl to another man, even though we weren't mar-ried then and still weren't after a two-year engagement. That was another story. Charles didn't seem to want to let go easily, didn't want to let go at all, even though the relationship between father and daughter never was all that strong. The problem was that the father was still treating the daughter like his little girl even though she was a grown woman, and a strong one at that. I thought I knew what was going on, and when I tried to explain it to Debra, she told me I was wrong. I thought she couldn't remove herself far enough from it to look at it objectively. So, there was always a lot of hurt going on between them, especially when Charles got a few drinks in him and tried to lay guilt off on Debra, but as she ma-tured, she learned to cope with it better.

I sat down on a chaise lounge in the shade and looked at the red rock in the corner. Dinner was served at four o'clock. By that time Charles had had three full tumblers of scotch and was quite drunk. He ordered Frances around and poked her with his knuckles and

Got no Secrets to Conceal

verbally abused her until she was almost crying. That seemed to be the pattern every time Debra and I went to San José to visit them. And every time we left, Debra would be so depressed.

Highway One, which was the main route from Santa Cruz to San José, was a treacherous stretch of road under any circumstances, and it always made me nervous and on edge. Our trip back to Santa Cruz was especially unnerving that day. I reached for the base of my neck and massaged it. I knew the pain I was feeling there was from stress. I was really looking forward to getting into bed alone that night. Debra dropped me off at my place and drove home. I slept soundly.

Seven

I was up early the next morning, did my usual two hundred sit-ups and made myself some breakfast. It was one of those foggy mornings with a mysterious quietude that I liked, although most of the time I thought the fog oppressive. This was an unusual sky for the time of year. Our foggy mornings typically came in the summer months. Fog is depressing whether it's in December or August. The only difference between the two months is that the fog is cold in winter. But it wasn't so cold that I wanted to skip my bike ride. I hadn't checked out the waves at the Lane in a while, and I wanted to do that. I was so distracted lately by thoughts of Renata that I hadn't been surfing as much as I liked to. That day was a good example. I *could* go check the waves, but there was no way I was going surfing. I was meeting Renata at one o'clock at the Terrace Court motel. So, the question was, why was I checking the waves if I wasn't going out? Because once you start following the surf, you never stop. So, I jumped on my bike and away I went.

After I looked at the surf, which wasn't great because it was too early, I peddled out to the end of the wharf. I turned right on Beach Street when I came off the wharf. As I passed the Terrace Court on my left, I wondered if we'd have a room with as nice a view as the one we had at the Casa Blanca.

Got no Secrets to Conceal

The phone was ringing as I unlocked the back door. It was a telephone solicitor selling medical insurance. I was definitely interested in his rap, always looking for a better deal than I had. That was one thing I'd never have to worry about after Debra and I got married. One of the fringe benefits of her teaching job was full medical insurance coverage for her and her dependents. I had a Blue Cross policy, for which I paid a monthly premium. It didn't cover much, major medical mostly. For me alone that was all I needed, and it only cost me something like fifty bucks a month. I wasn't sure how this solicitor was going to do better than that, but I listened to him anyway, and he really couldn't improve on what I had.

Renata called at one-fifteen.

"It's room 104," she said. "This one's not quite as nice as the Casa Blanca."

"I'm sure it'll be all right. You're go'n'a be there and that's all I care about."

"Oh, it's nice," she said. "It's just not quite like that other room. Listen, why don't you get down here."

"Okay, I'll be there in a few minutes," and I was out the door as soon as I hung up.

I entered the driveway from Beach Street, and as I approached the room, I saw right away the location wasn't as good as it was at the other motel. The other room had its own deck out the front door; this one was merely one in a row of anonymous doors that faced a parking lot. Walking up to the door, I was feeling exposed, as though a lot of people were watching me, which probably wasn't true because Renata's car was the

59

only one in the lot. Standing on a raised concrete side-walk and looking around after knocking on the door, I couldn't see anybody or tell if anybody could see me. From within, I heard her say,

"It's open. Come in."

So, I twisted the knob and entered the room. She was lying on the bed, propped up on pillows, a book in her hands. She set the book down on the bed, got up, walked over to me and hugged and kissed me.

"You weren't kidding about this room not being as nice as the other one," I said as we held each other.

"No, I wasn't, but it'll serve our purposes. Look, we even have a T.V. It takes quarters." She was now standing next to it. "I thought about turning it on for when you walked through the door. I know how much you love television, but then I thought better of it, and I didn't have any quarters anyway."

I was glad she didn't have any quarters. The last thing I wanted was to have a television set making a lot of noise. Nothing could be more annoying. Again, I be-gan the inevitable comparing and contrasting of Renata and Debra. I could get plenty of television hanging around with Debra, but the kind of sex that Renata had to offer was beyond all comparison. So, I thought it was worth the kidding about the television to be able to get such great sex.

"Come here," she said.

I walked over to her, kind of hangdog. I wanted to be with her, if I could only just be with her, but it seemed I couldn't. Rather I had to listen to some things I didn't want to hear to just be with her. She took me in

60

Got no Secrets to Conceal

her arms and hugged me and stroked the sides of my head with her soft, slim hands with long, red fingernails. Then she kissed me passionately. Before I knew what was happening, she was under me, on top of me, slamming into me, screaming and moaning ecstatically.

After we hit the sweet spot, we collapsed, exhausted, but oh so satisfied. As we recovered, we talked about what we'd been doing and how we'd been since the last time we were together. She'd been going to her class at the university. Final exams were coming up the following week. That would be the end of the quarter. She was following it up with one class in winter quarter and one in spring. She planned to go to at her graduation in June. In the meantime, she was going to keep working at her part-time job. She was also looking for another, better situation.

"There's something in the paper that looks interesting. I'm going to look into it. It's only four hours a day, something to do with senior community employment development, whatever that is. Leaves me enough time to take the last two classes I need to graduate. The office is in a house on Lincoln Street a couple blocks from your place. Bill doesn't think I ought'a bother with it, but at this stage, I'm pretty much ready to take anything. I've really got to make more than Ramona's paying me. It's been a good three years since I've had a real job, and I've been playing the housewife and mother role long enough now. Actually, four hours would be perfect in respects other than the money. I don't think Tess is quite ready to let me go completely. So, this would be a nice transition."

Jerome Arthur

"Kind of money they pay?" I asked.

"Who knows? I don't think very much, but better than Ramona's paying me. She doesn't give me enough hours to make anything. I'll sacrifice good pay to not have to travel over the hill into the pit. It's bad enough having one member of the family doing it, and I think that having both parents going over the hill every day would be hard on the kid, too."

"You're right there," I said.

"I don't think my spouse wants me to drive over the hill either. He worries about me too much as it is. He's always wanting to know what I'm doing. He asked me what I was doing today, and I told him I was having lunch with you. Not you specifically. I just said a friend."

I didn't say it, but the first thing that came to my mind was, did she tell him she was getting a motel room, too? I knew I shouldn't think such things, but I couldn't help it. Sometimes I wanted to throw something like that at her as quickly as the statement that provoked it had been made, but I controlled myself and never did and never would. When I tried to make love to her again, I struggled. I was feeling clumsy and semi impotent. For the first time with her, I was halfway glad when it was over. Suddenly there was a knock at the door, and we both froze, I more than she. We looked at each other. Finally she said,

"Who is it?"

"It's the manager," came the muffled response. "I have new curtains for this room. Would it be possible to put them in now?"

Got no Secrets to Conceal

"You can't do it now. Please come back later," Renata said.

"Sure. Sorry to disturb you."

And then he was gone. We both laughed as we heard the footsteps recede down the walkway.

"Reminds me of the time I had a room with a guy in Redwood City, and an ambulance came to the room next door. Sirens going, lights flashing, the works. I always remember how I was afraid they might want me and the guy I was with to be witnesses. Whatever happened in that motel room, I don't know, but they took somebody out on a stretcher. We were never asked to be witnesses."

"Were you married?" I asked, feeling suddenly innocent and artless.

"I wasn't, but he was," she shrugged and averted her eyes.

We both made one more half-hearted attempt to make love at around three-thirty. I needed to get out of there. As I was putting on my clothes, I was feeling fairly confused. I knew that something was happening, but I didn't know if it was that I was falling hopelessly in love with her, or if this was the beginning of the end, and I would soon not be seeing her at all. I told her that I'd talk to her soon. Maybe I'd call her on a day when she stayed home with her daughter. She told me that it would be nice, and she was looking forward to hearing from me. We hugged and kissed as I made my way to the door. I was back at my office within minutes. I sat down and thought. I couldn't get her out of my mind, yet

the thoughts and feelings I had were extremely disturb-
ing.

Eight

The Monday of the week before Christmas, Debra and I made our annual trip to San Francisco, where we had lunch at Tadich Grill and spent the afternoon Christmas shopping. A gray chill hung over the City like a shroud. Not my kind of weather at all. Debra didn't like the cold either, but for her it was tolerable because she really liked hanging out in the city.

On Wednesday, I called Renata at what I thought was a good time, when Bill would be gone to work, but she would still be home. She told me her parents would be flying in on Friday night and would stay until just before the new year. That meant she'd be busy entertaining and tending to them while they were in town, and I'd lose touch with her for a time.

"You been havin' a nice visit with your mom and dad?" I said.

"Oh yeah. We always do. I'm sure they'll spoil their granddaughter. I expect they'll fill this little house with Christmas presents for her. We'll be wading through them by the time it's over."

We chatted a while longer. She said she'd call me as soon as her parents left for home. Then she mentioned something about hugs and kisses and was gone. I heard the receiver click, and the finality of the sound made me shudder. For the next hour or so it was almost as if she didn't exist at all, had never existed. It was the first time that there was a set interval between times when we'd see each other. In the past it had always been, "I'll talk to you soon," and it was soon, or "I'll be in touch," and she was, but this time it was, "I won't talk to you until after the Christmas holidays." The specificity of such an impending commitment was encouraging. It was nice to know that I'd be talking to her at a definite time. That way, at least, I knew I'd be talking to her, but when it was left unspecified as it had been most of the time, I always entertained the possibility of never talking to her again.

Christmas came and went. Charles and Frances came to Santa Cruz in the early afternoon on Christmas Eve and stayed at Debra's place until late afternoon on Christmas Day. I arrived at about the same time they did and spent the afternoon and evening there, but not the night. Christmas day I got there early, had a nice time with Debra and her parents, and when they left, I stayed and spent the night with Debra.

I wondered what Renata was doing with her parents. She'd told me she had a good relationship with both her mother and father. She'd said on that first afternoon at the Casa Blanca that her father was the most important man in her life. I was touched by the sentiment. I remembered having a special affection for her when she'd said that, but then I also remembered what she'd said shortly after that. She had been trying to give me a physical description of her father and her brother. It seemed she was attracted to tall men, and she thought it was because both her father and brother were over six feet tall. She'd told me Bill was six/one. She finished the

66

Got no Secrets to Conceal

description of her brother by saying that she thought he was good looking in a different way.

"It would be easy for me to do something really taboo," she said. Then she went on and talked about her father, saying, "My dad is very handsome, and I might do something really taboo if the opportunity arose."

That little story brought that faraway look to her eyes once again.

Charles and Frances were in their car and gone by four o'clock on Christmas day. He wanted to get back over the hill before it got too dark. Debra and I lazed around the rest of the afternoon. No reason to go out. There was nothing happening in town. The Mall was like a ghost town.

I thought about Renata all through the week that followed Christmas. Any time I was anywhere near Beach Street, I sighed heavily. When I walked along West Cliff Drive in the chilly winter, I would recall the time she told me how when the surf crashed over the big rocks and cascaded down all sides, it reminded her of the best orgasm she'd ever had. Just thinking about her having an orgasm made me long for her, almost perversely. Indeed, these feelings seemed to be almost exclusively physical, but I was also beginning to miss her (not just her physical presence) when I didn't see her for a while. I felt like I couldn't wait till after the first of the year to see her again.

As a kind of lark, Debra suggested that we take off on New Year's Eve, maybe go south until we found some place we liked, get a motel and stay overnight. We ended up spending the night at a motel on a cliff overlooking the Pacific Ocean at Pismo Beach. It was a beautiful place and it was only twenty-five dollars a night. Same as the Casa Blanca. We had a delightful New Year's Eve dinner at a well-appointed steak and lobster restaurant with a view. I had lobster, my favorite; Debra had fillet mignon, bloody. We were sound asleep by ten o'clock. We had breakfast at a small diner around the corner from the motel and were checked out of the room by eleven o'clock on New Year's Day.

At ten o'clock on the second day of the New Year, Renata called me to touch base, as she put it. She told me that as soon as she got things back to normal following the holidays, she'd call me, and we could have lunch together. I now had something to look forward to. In another week we'd be talking to each other again; I'd have her in front of me. I could see her, maybe even get some hugs and kisses. I couldn't believe how much I was feeling and acting like an adolescent. The last time I remembered feeling like this was probably before Debra. The various conversations we'd had were coming back to me in bits and pieces. I'd recall something intimate Renata had told me about herself, and I'd reflect fondly upon her and our still-developing relationship. I'd think about something she said about how she liked her men, and then I'd match that to one or several of my own traits, and for the most part I was feeling just fine about myself, about her, and about what was going on between us. That's why I was completely unprepared for what she would tell me on our next lunch date.

Nine

We couldn't get our schedules coordinated enough to meet for lunch until the end of the month. Since I didn't have any of my own, I didn't know how all-consuming a little baby could be. Every time we came up with an earlier time, it was preempted, usually because of something to do with Tess. But then too I was always surprised at how much time Renata was able to arrange. I still wasn't very busy in the office, so my schedule was wide open. When the day finally came, I wanted it to be over with before it even started. I certainly wasn't prepared for any bad news.

We met for lunch at Positively Front Street, a hamburger and beer joint just around the corner from the two motels where we'd made love. I realized something was amiss as soon as I saw her. Her eyes glanced downward as I approached and hugged her. Her response was lackluster. It felt like I was embracing dead weight. She wasn't anything like she'd been the first time we were together. Even the second time was better than this, and it wasn't all that great.

We sat down at a table and ordered lunch. Our conversation was for the most part detached. The intimacy that had existed between us was gone. At one point she said in a very general way that when she was twenty-two, she was hot (pronounced "hhhot"), and I responded that she seemed pretty hot to me the last couple times we were together. She smiled, her eyes as faraway as I could ever remember seeing them. After some moments of deafening silence and small talk, chitchat, both of which were weighing heavily upon me, I asked her point blank when I could expect to see her again to make love. She stammered at the abruptness of the question.

"I don't know," she said, obviously thinking seriously about what she'd say next. "Something's happening to me. I'm experiencing a change. Right now, I only want to be with Bill. Maybe it's because I don't have a job of my own, or something. I don't know. Maybe when I get back out there again, I'll be looking around, but right now, I want to be faithful to him."

She didn't appear to me to be agonizing too much. It all seemed so arbitrary, as if her emotions were like a water faucet that she could turn on or off at the slightest impulse. At that moment I was feeling very confused. Vicissitudes. It was the first time I thought of the word and Renata simultaneously. It later became the word that always came into my mind when I was trying to explain her to myself.

"'Long may you run, although these changes have come,'" I said to her, quoting Neil Young. It was the only thing I could think of.

I didn't want to let her know how strongly I felt about her and how much I was hurting. I wanted to be out of there, so when we finished eating, I told her I had some things to do and that I would see her later. I walked her to her car, hugged and kissed her, and told her to take care of herself. Then I turned and walked away with a sighing anguish in my heart.

70

Got no Secrets to Conceal

It wouldn't take me long to reconcile myself to the fact that I wouldn't be her lover anymore, but for the moment I couldn't seem to concentrate on anything else. All afternoon I felt my heart stopping and starting. By the next day I was getting used to this new paradigm, but I still couldn't get her out of my mind, and the melancholy heart-pain continued.

Not two weeks passed before I heard from her again. She called only to talk to me, to see how I was doing, to see if I wanted to have lunch with her again. Of course, I wanted to have lunch with her. It was better than nothing. So, we arranged to meet the next day at Zoccolli's delicatessen.

It was the first week of February and the winter chill was hanging on, but the crystal-clear blue sky and yellow sun had their salutary and warming effects. The heavy rains were past, and little nubs mottled the trees and bushes. In less than a month, they would be blossoming and bursting forth in reds, pinks and whites. It was perfect walking weather. The morning of the day that I would meet her, I didn't make any effort to be clean shaven. At twelve noon I locked up the office and walked over to Pacific Avenue. As I approached, she was again waiting for me out in front. She stood up, advanced on me and gave me a hug, a real hug, a hug like old times.

"How have you been?" she asked as we walked into the delicatessen.

"Fine. how about yourself?"

"Great," she said. "Since I last talked to you, I got a job. It's only temporary, but it's full-time."

"Really. What kinda' job?"

"It's with the county. They need a clerical person to help in the emergency office. Basically I'm taking applications from people who need help because they sustained flood damage during the last big storm. It only pays six bucks an hour, but it's a good start, and it's only temporary. I'm in the basement of the county building, and you ought to see the guy who's my boss. He's been working in there a long time. His face looks like the cement basement we work in."

"How long's the job last?" I asked.

"Probably only the month of February, but I think I might be able to land something permanent later. The guy from the county administrative office, who walked me down to my job, asked me a lot of questions about my background and education. He said new positions are always coming up."

"Hmm. Wonder if that was Charles. I have this buddy, Charles Van Houten, works in the C.A.O.'s office."

"This guy's name's Charles, a small, wiry guy with dark hair and a southern accent."

"An in-your-face southern accent. Yep, that's Charles."

"Where's he from with that accent?"

"Grew up in Birmingham, Alabama. That's an Alabama accent. One of the funniest people I know. Yuh see 'im again, tell 'im I said hi."

"I will," she said.

We got our sandwiches and walked over to San Lorenzo Park and ate. We talked for about forty-five

Got no Secrets to Conceal

minutes and when we split up, she gave me another strong hug and she promised that she'd call me again soon.

Now that I knew that we wouldn't be lovers anymore, the time seemed to pass more quickly than it had when we were intimate, which, I guess, was a good thing because I really didn't want to be going through this misery in slow motion.

Another week went by and she was on the phone to me again. It was a Monday afternoon, and she wanted to meet me for a drink when she finished doing some things for Ramona. She was still putting in about an hour for her on Mondays after she got off from the county. I told her to meet me at the Oak Room at seven o'clock.

Then suddenly I found myself anticipating being with her again, and I had to bring myself back to reality. I was having a lot of anxiety. I had all this pent up feeling for her, yet I found that I had to restrain myself, had to calm myself, be cool. I wondered how I'd keep control when I was with her. As it turned out, I didn't have any problem with it. At a quarter to seven, I walked into the bar and ordered a beer. I knew the bartender, who wasn't busy, so we talked while I sipped my beer and waited for Renata. She came in at about five to seven and sat down next to me.

"This is an interesting place," she said. "First time I've been here."

"Really? It's a cool bar," I said and then I introduced her to James, the bartender.

They exchanged greetings, and she ordered a shot of The Glenlivet scotch with a water back. Because it was Monday, nobody else was in the bar, so James hung out with us. After a little while, some people came in and that took him away. That's when she told me about a guy she'd met at Ramona's house earlier. The guy was a financial adviser, and he was going over Ramona's books with Renata.

"He asked me out for a drink. I don't think I want to do that, because I know the guy wants something more than just to have a drink."

"You think so?" I said.

"Oh, no doubt about it," she replied.

"Well, you can always go out with me anytime, and I promise it'll only be for whatever you want it to be for."

She seemed to hesitate before she said it, but her meaning was clear when she told me, "You can have more than just a drink with me."

I raised an eyebrow, as I'd done on an earlier occasion, and said, "No kidding? Don't wan'a be faithful to your spouse anymore?"

"I told you things might change if I got a job. Well, that's happened. At the end of the month when the temporary job ends, I'm going to work for the county's health clinic on Freedom Boulevard in Watsonville. I think your friend Charles might've helped. So, things've changed with my job situation, and I'm feeling pretty free and easy at this point, and besides, I've found that I just can't stay away from you. I think you might be different from anyone I've ever met."

"Wow. These last couple months have been really hard," I said. I didn't want to seem overanxious and

Got no Secrets to Conceal

give too much away. I was restraining myself and it was hard. "So, yuh wan'a get together again?"

"I think so but I don't know when right now. Let me get organized on this new job and we'll go from there. Right now, I've got to be getting home. It's getting past the time when Bill will be expecting me."

James could see that we were getting ready to leave, so he came over to say goodbye.

"I hope I'll be seeing you again," he said to Renata, extending his hand to her. She shook it and said,

"You will," and I had a flash of jealousy until I heard her say, "You'll be seeing me with Jack again sometime."

We left the bar and I walked her to her car. She was parked around the corner in a public lot next to the county jail. I embraced her and kissed her passionately, running my hands down her back so that they rested on her soft haunches. As I fondled them gently, she said,

"Please don't. I don't like grab-assing in public, and besides what about those guys up there," gesturing to the upper floors of the jail.

"The hell with them," I said softly, still hugging her. "They can go jack off for all I care." We both chuckled and she got into her car. I kissed her one more time, and she drove off.

Ten

On Friday she called me to see if we could meet at the Casa Blanca on Monday. She said she'd be at Ramona's for about an hour after work that first day on her new job.

"Seven o'clock be okay?" she asked. "Like the other night at the bar?"

"Perfect. See yuh then."

She gave me the phone number of her new job. I already had Ramona's number, so there wouldn't be any problem getting in touch with her if I had to. As soon as she hung up, time started to drag again. The next three days would be an infinity.

The weekend passed and on Monday after school, Debra called to tell me she needed my help that evening. She was rearranging the furniture in her townhouse and wanted me to help her move it around.

"Can you come up and give me a hand?" she said.

"Sure," I said, not even thinking about my date with Renata.

Disappointment set in when I realized I'd have to break that date. I called her at work and after I explained the situation to her, she said,

"How about next Monday? You want to meet me then? It'll be hard to wait another week, but I guess I'll have to."

Got no Secrets to Conceal

"Uh, let's see, uh, I don't know," I stammered. "Yeah I guess so. Let me think."

"Are you okay?" she asked.

"Yeah, I'm okay. Just disappointed about today, and not sure about next week. I don't know if I can wait that long either, but yeah let's go for it."

"We can do it. You'll see."

"Wan'a meet at the same time as we were go'n'a meet today?"

"I think so. I've been going to Ramona's house on Mondays and putting in an hour or so after I get off from my day job, so that should work out all right. Seven o'clock next Monday. We'll talk more next week. I won't make it through the week without talking to you at least once."

"Okay. Sorry about today. Can't wait to talk to you again."

"Me too. Hugs and kisses," she said and hung up. Debra had invited me up to her place for dinner before we started to move stuff around. I took along a bottle of Beringer zinfandel. I was a little out of sorts because of the broken date with Renata, and apparently I wasn't hiding it.

"Are you okay, honey?" Debra asked. "You seem preoccupied."

"I'm okay," I lied. I couldn't very well tell her the truth. "Just a little worried about the business is all. Only got three jobs going on right now, your dad, and two insurance companies. Not much on the horizon. I think I might advertise in the paper. Yellow pages ad doesn't seem to be doing much."

Jerome Arthur

"I hope you start getting a little more successful. It's no fun watching you mope around."

"I'll be okay. Run some ads, get some business and I'll be doing better."

After dinner we spent a couple hours moving furniture around, and when things met her satisfaction, we relaxed and finished off the wine. Then I spent the night with her and went back to my place in the morning.

The next week went by ever so slowly. Renata called on Wednesday, and we set the final arrangements for our Monday date.

"Can you reserve the room, and I'll meet you there at around seven o'clock? I'll be too busy with my two jobs to do it."

"I'll take care of it," I said.

"How about if you bring me a beer or something. I could've used one last Monday after the busy day I had, and I know I'm going to want one come next Monday."

"No problem. See yuh then."

I went to the Casa Blanca at about two o'clock on the big day and paid twenty-five dollars cash for room twenty-four. The woman at the desk wanted to know the license number of my car. I told her I'd come into town on the Greyhound and wasn't driving. I also said I'd left my luggage in a locker at the bus station, and I'd go back and get it later. I signed the register, got the key and went to the room. After checking it out, I took a walk along West Cliff out to the lighthouse and back to my office. I called Renata and told her we had the same room as before. Then I spent the rest of the afternoon doing some paperwork. I got back to the room at six-thirty.

Suddenly I remembered the beer, so I went down the stairs to Beach Street and walked the one block to Beach Liquors and bought a couple bottles of Beck's and went back to the room. I'd brought the Rossner novel, so I propped myself up on the bed and began to read. I left the door ajar so that when Renata got there, she could walk right in, which she did a few minutes after I'd gotten the beer. I bounded off the bed and gave her an enthusiastic hug and kiss. She was receptive, but I could tell she was tired. It had been her first day of the second week on her new job, and she put in a little over an hour at Ramona's. She looked beat, but she said she'd be fine after she got a breath of fresh air and a shower. I stood back and watched with appreciation her silhouetted figure go out the door. She stood by the metal railing with her back to me, her arms splayed with her hands on the rail. As she looked out on the bay and wharf, a breeze blew her long hair away from her face. The dress she wore fluttered languorously around her. I was so happy to see her like this again.

After a few minutes I joined her, and she explained how hectic her day had been. She said she was happy to be with me again. She hugged and kissed me, and then slipped out of my arms and back into the room where she took off her clothes and got into the shower. I closed the door and the curtains.

The room was cozy enough without having to turn on the heater. There were no walls with right angles

79

in the room. It was an interesting design. I liked it, and as Renata and I used it, I developed a kind of possessive attachment to it, a connection that was developing even as I lay there at that moment. In fact, the next time I referred to it, I would call it "our room," and she would smile her faraway smile. I was sure she approved, and everything was and would be wonderful.

I could see her outline through the translucent glass shower door. She moved easily and unhurriedly, spreading the soap around and then rinsing it off. I breathed deeply and was so satisfied at that moment. Coming out of the shower, she undid her long hair and let it fall over her shoulders. The towel was wrapped around her torso, and when she got to the side of the bed, she let it drop to the floor.

"I'm thinking about getting my hair cut. How do you feel about it? Something quite a bit shorter than this. I know Bill won't like the idea, but how do *you* feel?"

"You'd look good with short hair," I replied.

"Thirty's too old for this kind of length. When a woman reaches that age, and she's got long hair, she probably thinks it makes her look young. The opposite is true. Besides, short hair is so much easier to deal with than long hair. I'm getting too busy to be spending a lot of time on it."

She held her hair back to suggest a shorter style.

"Everything you said is true, and I think you'll look very attractive with it shorter."

"I'm going to do it. Now, why don't you get out of those clothes and into something more comfortable, like nothing."

80

Got no Secrets to Conceal

Then she slid up next to me and helped me with my clothes. And for the next three hours, we performed (and I don't mean just singing) some lyrics straight out of the Warren Zevon songbook:

> "We made mad love, shadow love, random love and abandoned love…"

It was after this rendezvous that I was pretty sure I was in love with her, but I didn't tell her, not yet. And what was I going to do about Debra? Our engagement? How was I going to break the news to her? And how would Renata respond? If I told her I was in love with her, would she reciprocate? Things were getting complicated.

At around ten o'clock when it was time for Renata to be getting home, I asked her to drop me off in front of the Cooper House. I wanted to sit in a bar for a few minutes to contemplate my satisfaction and self content. When she dropped me off, she waited until I was almost to the front door of the bar before she pulled away from the curb. I noticed this, and when I looked over my shoulder, I saw her staring at me, and I couldn't describe the look on her face (I didn't know what to call it), but it sure made me feel good to see her looking at me like that.

I went into the bar and ordered a Glenlivet and a water back because it reminded me of her. I hadn't really drunk any hard liquor to speak of since my early twenties, restricting myself to beer mostly with occasional periods of various jug burgundies or rosés. I sat at the end of the bar closest to the window where I had a view of the deserted street. The bar was pretty much deserted too. There were two guys sitting at the bar. James was busy washing glasses and cleaning up. I savored the warm, heavy, peaty smell of The Glenlivet. Leaning on the bar and peering out the window, I watched winter going into its last stages. Spring was less than three weeks away. It was long overdue.

Eleven

The rapid succession of events that followed threatened to overtake me, but before that could go down, the pace decelerated so abruptly that I felt like a sailboat in irons when it happened. But that was later. She took time out of her busy schedule to call me on Tuesday just "to hear the sound of your voice." This moved me to call her Wednesday morning to see if she could meet me for lunch at El Ranchero, a Mexican restaurant on Main Street in Watsonville.

"Absolutely!" she sighed breathlessly without hesitation. "I can hardly wait to *see* you again!"

"Me too! What time you wan'a meet, and where?"

"I should be able to get to the restaurant a little after one. I'll meet you there," she said and hung up.

The bus ride to Watsonville usually took about an hour, but mine took a little longer than that because of a problem on the route. In fact, at one point, I worried that I might not make it in time to meet her.

At Cabrillo College, one of the passengers, an elderly woman, keeled over in her seat, prompting the driver to call for an ambulance. We had about a fifteen-minute delay which was making me a little nervous and impatient. I didn't want to miss any time with Renata, but I also tried to be kind and considerate. After all, she was an old woman, and there might be something seriously wrong with her. The paramedics took her away.

In the meantime, I bore my patience by thinking how Renata had once said that the average person doesn't have a lot of patience with little kids and old people. She was referring to one time when she was crossing the street with Tess, and how she wasn't going to rush her kid or pick her up and carry her just because of some impatient driver. I thought she would be pleased with me for the way I played it on the bus.

As soon as we got onto Freedom Boulevard, the driver started to make up for lost time, going forty-five to fifty miles an hour on some stretches. We got to the end of the line at five to one, perfect timing.

I got out and walked the long block to El Ranchero, and seeing that Renata had not arrived yet, sat down on a bus stop bench at the corner. I saw her driving down Main Street a block away. She turned the corner without seeing me and headed toward the parking lot behind Woolworth.

As I stood up, there was a loud screech of skidding tires. Two cars crashed in the intersection. One of the drivers had run the red light at about thirty miles an hour and broadsided the other car. No one seemed to be hurt, but both drivers were shaken. Renata came out the front door of Woolworth completely unaware of the accident. A crowd had gathered, and she walked right into the middle of it. I had to flag her down, and as we walked to the restaurant, I told her what happened.

"How's your new job?" I asked after we were seated in the restaurant.

Got no Secrets to Conceal

"If nothing else, at least interesting," she replied. "I think I'm going to like it. It only pays eight bucks an hour, so I'll keep my eyes open for other, better paying county jobs. This job's okay. I'm working with some nice ladies. How've you been?"

"Just fine. Now that we're seeing each other again, things have really improved. Didn't even mind the hour-long bus ride, 'cause I knew I was go'n'a be seeing you at the end of it. And now here you are, and everything is just fine."

"That's funny. I've been having the same feelings. So, you think maybe we can get together Saturday? I'm going over to Ramona's for about an hour on Saturday. I was thinking maybe one o'clock. I thought it might be nice to get together after that, maybe for a drink. What do you think?"

"Great idea. Let's do it."

I had two chile verde burritos, and she had a taco and chicken enchilada combination. As we were eating, she told me a little about her job and a couple of the part-time ladies she worked with. One of them (they were both American/Mexicans) had already confided in her that she thought her husband was having an affair. Renata was her supervisor.

"The supervisor part of my job will look good on my résumé," she said.

"No doubt."

"And I'm flattered by Leticia's trust to confide in me, especially since I've only known her a few days."

Over the next few months that Renata worked there, I would be hearing stories about Leticia. She would be in and out of Renata's favor over the months, caused by various domestic problems that she let affect her job performance. I was sure that Renata was usually justified in her criticism of Leticia, but I also knew that she could be a stern taskmaster. She was the kind of person who played hardball no matter what she did. She told me on more than one occasion that she was a hard-hearted person, and she proved it, too, by telling me about her many sexual exploits when she knew (or did she?) how much it bothered me. I couldn't imagine what it must be like to work for her or to be married to her and submit to it from the point of view of employee or spouse. I wondered how much she told Bill and how he took it. She said that he showed very little interest in any of her affairs, and the way she said it sounded like she told him about them. But I could never be sure how much Bill knew about Renata's activities when she wasn't with him, how much he knew because she told him or how much he knew without her telling him anything. I thought about these things as we ate and talked, but I never did come up with any answers to the questions that puzzled me so, and I never would.

At ten to two, we started gathering up our things. We paid the check, and left the restaurant, heading toward her car. She suggested that I catch the bus from the shopping center across the street from the county annex where she worked. That gave me less time on the bus and more time with her, so I got into her car and we were on our way to her office. As we turned the corner to go into her parking lot, I could see that my bus was already in the shopping center, so I asked her to pull over,

Got no Secrets to Conceal

and I'd get out right there. She turned into her parking lot and stopped. Before I got out, I leaned across and gave her a big hug and a long kiss. We agreed that we'd see each other on Saturday.

I jogged over to the bus, and it pulled out immediately as soon as I boarded it. The ride back to Santa Cruz was uneventful, and as seem all return trips, quicker than going. I got off the bus at the stop at the triple deck parking lot next to the movie theaters by the river. That made for a nice walk back to my office, which was certainly better than sitting on a bus in the rumbling congestion of downtown.

By the time I got back to my office, it was already three-fifteen. I'd been gone three and half hours. I listened to the two messages on my answering device. They were insurance company representatives seeking my services. I set up an appointment to meet with one of them that afternoon, and the other the next day.

Twelve

Friday morning, I called Renata and confirmed our date for Saturday. She was going over to Ramona's at noon for about an hour, and afterward we'd meet at the Oak Room for a drink.

"Really looking forward to it," I said.

"Me too."

"What're the chances we can skip the drink and get cuarto veinticuatro de Casa Blanca? Make some serious love."

It was a shot in the dark, and I knew realistically that it wasn't going to happen. Debra and I had a dinner date that night, so I knew my time with Renata would be short.

"Not tomorrow, but soon. I'm just as eager as you."

"Okay," I said, and we broke the connection.

I had to keep reminding myself that she was married and had a whole other life. The same was almost true for me. Debra and I weren't married yet, but we might as well have been, for as many years as we'd been going together and been engaged. I was feeling more and more like I was just putting in time with Debra. Routine time. It was becoming clear to me we had different values and interests. Those differences hadn't been so noticeable when we first met and during the early years of the relationship. And of course, my judgment was col-

Got no Secrets to Conceal

ored by my recent attachment to Renata. Comparisons were unavoidable, and when I saw Debra do or say something that I didn't agree with, I looked to Renata to see what she thought about the same subject. Usually her opinion was similar to mine, or at least it was different from Debra's. This only made me more critical of Debra. Probably the biggest difference between the two women was their attitudes toward sex and it's importance to a person's psychological well being.

At about seven-thirty that evening, I decided to walk over to Lulu Carpenter's on Pacific Avenue. It was a small saloon with stained glass and potted plants. In those days they called them fern bars. I wanted to get out and see what people were doing. I really hadn't been to a bar by myself lately. The last time I was at the Oak Room, I was with Renata, and I would be with her there again tomorrow.

It took me about ten minutes to get to Lulu's. I walked into the waning drunkenness of happy hour. People who'd been there since five o'clock were slurring the evening away. Some who had arrived later only had a glow. The happy hour crowd was thinning out. I found a table along the wall opposite the bar and sat down facing the front door so that I could watch the incoming traffic. The Giants and Dodgers played mutely on the television over the end of the bar. The Modern Jazz Quartet played dreamily on the stereo. Within a half hour I was virtually alone in the bar. Toward the back was a couple in intimate tableau at one of the candlelit tables. Two guys were sitting separately at the bar. The bartender washed glasses and cleaned up behind the bar,

89

Jerome Arthur

and the cocktail waitress picked up glasses and wiped tabletops. I sipped on my Beck's beer and read my novel, looking occasionally toward the front to see who might be passing by on the street. I was there long enough for one beer.

I walked the full length of the Mall, which was bustling with movie and restaurant patrons. The book and record stores were a-swarm with some browsers and buyers. People milled around the front door of the Catalyst. The line to the box office went halfway down the block. Jackson Browne's name was on the marquee. Tampico Kitchen, one block farther down, was bulging at the seams with late diners drinking margarita's and listening to a guitar trio. I went through Bonesio's liquor store parking lot to Laurel. In contrast to Pacific, Laurel, had nothing but car traffic racing east to west, west to east. I was the only pedestrian in sight. I turned right on Center and walked the two blocks up to my house. I went to bed that night filled with anticipation for tomorrow's date.

Thirteen

I was awake before dawn. I liked sunrise at that time of year. The first day of spring was eight days earlier, and daylight savings time had just kicked in. I checked the tide chart in the paper as I ate breakfast. There was a -0.3 low tide at 6:45 a.m. I finished my breakfast, and at seven o'clock, I got on my bike and headed down to Cowell's Beach to check it out. It was looking good, so I went back to the house and got ready to go surfing.

I got out of the water at around noon and went straight home to get ready to meet Renata at the Oak Room. I got there at a little before one. The band that usually played weekends on the patio was just finishing its first set as I approached. Renata was coming toward me from the opposite direction. We met at the entrance to the patio.

"How yuh doin'?" I asked as we made our way up the steps to the front door of the restaurant.

"Good, especially now that you're here."

She looped her arm through mine and hugged my shoulder to her cheek. I was oblivious of anybody who might have been watching us. For all I cared at that moment, Debra could have been standing right there.

"How yuh been?" I asked as we took our seats at the bar.

Jerome Arthur

"New job's keeping me busy. I like the work and the people I work with. I just wish it paid more fort the work they're asking me to do. Bill's getting a little anxious. He really hates his job. Wants to quit, but I've got to be making almost as much as he makes for it to be practical, and I'm almost there. He makes ten bucks an hour and I only make eight. It's close. What I'm doing right now is just a start. Something better will come along. I know it will."

"That's great. Bet it feels good to be working, getting your own money for a change."

"Yes indeed. I don't think there's anything more demoralizing for a woman than being at the mercy of some man for the money she needs to do the things she wants to do. Being a housewife is okay, but there's just no money in it. It's the only full-time job I can think of that doesn't pay anything."

"Boy, you said a mouthful there."

"So, how've you been?" she asked.

"All right. Been pretty busy, too" I lied. I wasn't busy at all. "Went out last night to see what was happenin'. Not much was. I wasn't out more'n two hours. Boring. Lota' people. Nothin' happenin'."

James wasn't behind the bar, and the guy tending bar tuned the radio to the country music station KFAT during the live music break. This surprised me because the music, whether live or not, at the Cooperhouse was usually jazz. Jerry Jeff Walker was singing "Jaded Lover."

"Here, listen to this," I said. "This is a cool song."

Got no Secrets to Conceal

We quit talking and listened. When it ended, I asked her what she thought.

"It kind of reminds me of me, and the end of some of the affairs I've had," she said.

Suddenly I wished I hadn't called her attention to the song because I didn't want to hear her say that, but it was too late now, and it gave me a pain that I didn't want to have at that time, just when I was feeling good about her and me and what was going on between us. These flippant comments from her always made me feel lousy, but I swallowed hard and forged ahead.

"You think so?" I shouldn't have asked.

"I know so." And her eyes crackled from those flinty dark pupils out to the edges of her two-tone irises.

"So, how did it go over at Ramona's house?" I asked to change the subject.

"Pretty good. She wasn't there, so I got a lot done. It usually works that way. When she's around, we usually end up talking. Tells me her troubles and I try to console her."

"Really? Doesn't sound to me like she should have any troubles. What kinda' troubles?"

"All kinds. She'll get in a relationship with a guy, usually one who's quite a bit younger, and she'll really care for the guy, and he'll be going along just because she has money and will take care of him. I've seen this happen three times in the year and a half that I've known her. She's always depressed, and she drinks too much and uses drugs, cocaine mostly, and prescription drugs. Other than that, she doesn't have any problems."

93

"Wow, I didn't know she was so screwed up. I wonder why."

"I think it goes back to her childhood. She's been addicted to diet pills since her early teens. I think her weight problem is the root of all her other problems. She's a pretty woman, and the fact that she's overweight makes her feel not so beautiful, so she takes drugs to pump herself up, but all that does is make her more depressed. And then her mother lays a lot of guilt on her. She's always criticizing her for being overweight. In fact, it was her mother who made her a diet pill junkie."

"No kiddin'. 'Sounds like she's a mess."

"She is, and sometimes it's hard to keep track of the men who float through her bed. I think I've finally met someone who's had as many men as I've had. Like the summer after my first year in college. I'd go out with a guy, and when he'd drop me off at my apartment, I'd have to ask *him* if he'd like to get a little nooky, and he'd usually respond that he wasn't thinking about it, but since I mentioned it, why not? And that seems to be how it is with Ramona, but she can't seem to handle it emotionally. She wants it, and when she gets it, she feels bad and cheap. I don't get it, but I try to console her."

"Why are you always telling me about how much sex you've done?" I blurted out. "What makes you think I wan'a hear about it?"

"Uh, I really hadn't thought about it," she said, seemingly taken aback. "It just seemed to be part of the conversation. Does it bother you?"

"Just a little," I said, a bit defensively.

94

Got no Secrets to Conceal

What started out to be a pleasant visit was turning into a confrontation. Suddenly I felt like all the progress we'd been making in the past few days was dwindling away.

"Have you noticed that I never tell you anything about my sex life? Reason I don't is 'cause it's nobody's business but mine, and it only concerns me and whomever else I get involved with, and that's how I feel about that."

"Too bad," she said.

For the next few minutes we stared silently through the liquor bottles at our reflections in the mirror behind the bar, she sipping her Glenlivet, I taking periodic swallows from my Beck's. The silence was what we needed. In a short time, we began talking again.

The band was playing again. I looked out the window at them and saw Charles Van Houten on the sidewalk. When we made eye contact, I waved him into the bar. He made his way through the crowd.

"Check it out, Renata," I said. "Charles."

"Oh, yeah. I remember him."

He came in and sat on a barstool on the other side of Renata. We were both turned toward her.

"Hi, there," he said to her. He had a quizzical look on his face.

"Renata Lowell. Remember, you introduced me to my boss my first day at work at the county."

"Oh, yeah."

"'T's happenin', brother?" I said. "What're yuh drinkin'?"

"Shot a' Jack Daniels. I'll get it," he said as the bartender approached. "What're you guys up to?"

"Not much. Just havin' a drink."

I glanced in the bartender's glass and saw Debra passing by the door of the bar. She looked right at Renata and me, looked away and continued going toward the rear of the Cooperhouse to the toy store, but not for long. Suddenly she popped back into the doorframe and came in.

"Hi," she said.

Renata swiveled in my direction on the barstool so that our knees were almost touching. Debra's eyes went back and forth between her and me.

"Hi. Oh, this is Renata," I stammered. "You know Charles, right?"

"Hello, Charles. Nice to see you again. How do you do, Renata? Nice to meet you." Then to me, "I was going to the toy store to get something for Julie's little boy."

"'Sounds good. Got something in mind?"

"Not really. Got'a go back and look around. I'm sure I'll find something. We still going out to dinner tonight?"

"Absolutely. I'll expect yuh at my place at six."

"All right. I'll see you then."

She exchanged pleasantries with Charles and Renata, turned and walked out. The tension was so thick you could cut it with a knife.

"Well, I guess it's time for me to be getting home," Renata said. "Bill's been watching the kid. Said

96

Got no Secrets to Conceal

he wanted to come downtown to Odyssey Records. He wants to get the latest Dire Straits album."

She'd told me before that her spouse had an elaborate stereo system and was particular about his record collection.

"Okay," I said, not offering any resistance. I think I inadvertently glanced in the direction of the toy store. "Take care. We got'a do this again sometime." I didn't want it to sound too obvious to Charles, but that strategy was no good.

"So, what's up?" he said after she'd left the bar. "You and Renata got something goin'?"

"That obvious, huh? Yuh think Debra picked up on it?"

"I don't see how she could miss it."

"That obvious."

"Let's put it this way—there's go'n'a be fireworks at the dinner table tonight

We didn't say any more about it as we finished our drinks and left.

Debra and I didn't argue that night at the dinner table. We were in the Crepe Place on North Pacific, and there was a crowd. She was too hurt to be angry. She'd driven down to my place, and we'd walked to the restaurant. She was supposed to be spending the night with me. Since the incident in the bar earlier, I wasn't so sure if she was still going to do it.

"So, who was your friend in the bar today?" she said without inflection as we walked back to my place.

"She works at the county. Charles showed her to her office on her first day on the job."

"You trying to tell me she was with Charles and not you?"

"She was with both of us. She's got another job, part-time in a private home on Beach Hill. Just happened to stop in the Oak Room for a drink on her way home to her husband and daughter up in the Valley. Charles and I were surprised to see her."

"Really?" Her look was skeptical.

"Really," was all I could say.

That was the end of the conversation for now. I had a feeling that it wasn't the final end, though.

Fourteen

On Monday Renata and I spoke on the phone twice. She called me in the morning, and I called her in the afternoon, and it went like that for the rest of the week. We were acting like a couple teenagers. She was settling into her job, but she was still very busy, so she had little time to spend with me. She was missing her time with Tess, and I understood that. In fact, I wondered how she managed to spend as much time with me as she did.

By the end of the week, Debra and I started planning our annual trip to Reno. We planned it for the weekend before Easter. For as long as we'd been together, we'd go up there in springtime. No beauty like the desert in bloom. The first year we were going together, we took a trip up that way with some friends who had an International Harvester Scout. We went up on a Friday, spent the night in a motel in Reno, and Saturday afternoon went out to a place called Alkali Flat not far from Fallon. There we did some light off-road driving and slept under the stars Saturday night. Early Sunday morning we headed home.

That was the only time we did anything as rugged as that. It was a great trip and we had a lot of fun. So, we decided to do it every year, just the two of us, minus the off-road stuff. Instead, we'd spend a couple nights in a different hotel/casino each time. We'd drive out to the desert on the second day, watch the sunrise and look at the blossoming desert flowers and cacti. In the afternoon, I'd play some blackjack and Debra would do some shopping. Then we'd head home the next morning.

"You sure you want to go to Reno this year," Debra asked after we'd already set the trip up.

"Of course. Why're you asking me that?"

"Oh, I don't know. You seem distracted lately. I find you in a bar with another woman. What am I supposed to think?"

"I'm telling you. Charles and I were both hangin' with her. She's just a friend. Works at the county with Charles."

"Okay," she replied, a skeptical look on her face.

"Hey, we're goin' to Reno. Go'n'a hang out a couple days, check out the wildflowers, do some gambling (you can go shopping), swim some laps in the pool at Harrah's. Just have a good time."

I don't know how convincing I was, but she seemed reassured, and that ended the conversation.

Even though I really wanted to be with Renata, hang out with her, make love to her, I was looking forward to the trip with Debra. I was still very much in love with her and wanted to spend some alone time with her on the desert. At that moment, Renata's sexual prowess was taking control. Yes, I did love Debra, but I was quickly falling deeply in love with Renata.

I always thought Reno was a cool town. It had a touch of the old west, but then there was all that glitter and neon. Not as much as Las Vegas, but plenty intense

100

Got no Secrets to Conceal

all the same. We'd be leaving the following Sunday morning. I'd talked to Renata the Friday before.

"I'll be thinking about you while I'm gone," I said. "I wish I was going with you instead of Debra."

"Likewise," she replied. "There'll be plenty of time for us when you get back."

Before we hung up, we set up a lunch date for Wednesday, which would be my first full day back home.

"I'll take the bus out to Watsonville," I said. "We can meet at El Ranchero again. That sound cool?"

"'Sounds great! Same time?"

"Sure. See yuh then." And we hung up.

Sunday morning came and Debra and I were on the road by nine o'clock. I drove to Sacramento where we stopped for lunch. From Sacramento Debra took the wheel and we got to Harrah's in Reno by two o'clock. It was late enough in springtime so that when we crossed the mountains and high desert, the temperature wasn't bad.

After we got checked in, I put on my swim trunks, Debra her two-piece bathing suit, and we went down to the pool. We got in and swam some laps. That was one thing I always liked about Debra. She was moderately athletic and didn't mind swimming a few laps in a pool or hiking out on the desert to look at the wildflowers and take in the aromas. She was physically active. After we got out of the pool, we went to our room and made love before napping. When we woke up, we got ready for dinner.

Jerome Arthur

After supper we got into my year-old Honda Civic and rode out to the desert to watch the sunset. When darkness fell on the landscape, Reno looked like a jewel shimmering in the distance. Stars filled the night sky, Orion, the Dippers, big and little, Arcturus, Polaris.

We couldn't see any of those heavenly bodies as we drove down Virginia Street back to Harrah's. The neon burned bright. Though the sky was dark, the brightness of it all made it seem like daylight.

I thought about Renata. It wasn't the first time since we'd left home. I wondered what she was doing right then. Probably sitting in front of the television with her family. Or could she be out with someone else? The thought crossed my mind, but then I dismissed it. I knew she'd be home on Sunday night, but how about tomorrow night? Might she leave Ramona's house and go over to the Oak Room and visit with James. This thought made me jealous. She had commented how lovely she thought his black skin was. I put these thoughts out of my mind. They made me crazy, but I couldn't stop thinking about her.

It was still early, but we were exhausted by then, so we went straight back to the hotel and got ready for bed.

It was dark when I woke up in the morning. Debra was still asleep. I got out of bed, put on my clothes and went out to the car. The sky in the east was changing colors. I could see it go from black to purple as I drove through the spring morning. Within ten minutes I was out on the desert. I drove out on a gravel road and pulled over to the side. I got out and sat on the hood.

102

Got no Secrets to Conceal

After only a few minutes, I got back into the car because it was so cold outside, and I hadn't brought a sweater or jacket with me. The sun was fully over the horizon after about forty-five minutes. I was astonished by the beauty of the sunrise on the desert. Almost as breathtaking as the sunrise at Cowell's Beach. Purple sage was everywhere, roosters were crowing, and periodically I could see a car off in the distance on some other gravel road trailing dust. When the sun was up, I started the car and headed back into town.

When I got to the hotel, Debra was up and about. She'd showered and was blowing her hair dry when I came in.

"Where yuh been?" she asked when she turned the blow dryer off.

"Went out to catch the sunrise. Been gone since before sunup. It *was* pretty. Can't wait to get back out there after breakfast."

"Mm, me too."

I took a shower and we went down to the ninety-nine-cent buffet in the hotel. After breakfast we went back to the room, read the newspaper and hung around till about ten o'clock. We wanted to beat the midday heat, so we headed out to the desert at that time. Like I said before, there aren't too many things in this world that are prettier than the desert in bloom. We hiked around for a couple hours until the temperature started going up. Reno's heat isn't nearly as oppressive as Las Vegas', but it can get up there, and it was doing it that day. We got back into town at half past noon, took showers and went down to the pool. We did a few laps and went to the room, made love again, and napped till about four o'clock.

"I'm going shopping," she said, as she freshened up in the bathroom. "Wan'a go?"

"Not really. Maybe I'll go play some blackjack. See if I can win something. Ha, ha."

"That's what I thought. Where you wan'a meet for dinner? And what time?"

"How 'bout Harrah's Steak House downstairs? We can meet here. Say seven o'clock? That'll give you a couple hours for shopping."

"'Sounds like a plan."

We left together, split up in the casino, and I went looking for a two-dollar blackjack table. I wasn't much of a gambling man, and certainly not a high roller. I figured I could afford to lose twenty-five bucks, and that was it. I found a table with only one other player and an attractive young woman dealer. After about an hour's play, I was up a hundred dollars, so I decided to quit while I was ahead.

I still had another hour before I was to meet Debra, so I took off for a walk up Virginia Street. I found her in a women's apparel store looking at blouses. She had a small, flat bag with postcards in it.

"Win anything?" she asked as I approached.

"About a hundred bucks. How 'bout you? You spend that much?"

"Not even close to that much. Here, take a look."

She took the cards out of the bag and showed them to me.

Got no Secrets to Conceal

"This one'll be for mom and dad."

She showed all of them to me and told me where they were going. Then she held up the blouse she was looking at and asked me what I thought. It was a plain, salmon colored blouse. Very nice. Her color and style. I told her to go ahead and buy it.

"So, shall we just go straight to dinner? It's a quarter to seven."

"Sure, let's go."

"Let me take these things up to the room. We can freshen up while we're there."

"'Sounds good. 'S go."

And so ended our trip to Reno. We had dinner, went to the bar for after-dinner drinks and back to our room. We were in bed by nine o'clock. We made love one last time and fell asleep.

Fifteen

The trip home was uneventful. I thought about Renata the whole way. When we got back to Santa Cruz on Tuesday afternoon, I was so anxious to see her on Wednesday that I was getting jumpy. I called her first thing in the morning.

"Hi, how yuh doin'?"

"Oh, hi," she said softly. I sensed an excitement in her husky, Bacall-sounding voice. "I've missed you and can't wait to see you at lunchtime."

"Yeah, I've missed you too, and can't wait either," I replied."

"How was your trip?"

"Had a good time. We only went to Reno, so it was short but sweet. I've missed you. I'm thinking about you all the time."

"Well, I don't know if I'm thinking about you that much, but I do think about you a lot. Not much change around here. Starting to settle in on this job, and I like it a lot. Oop, I've got a call here on another line. Got to go."

"Okay. See yuh in a bit."

"Okay. Bye."

"Bye."

Got no Secrets to Conceal

I was busy trying to catch up with my work. I was now working on three insurance cases, and still had some work to do for Charles Morrison. Keeping busy relieved some of the tension I was feeling. By eleven o'clock I started getting ready to walk over to Metro Center to catch a bus to Watsonville. But that trip was not to happen. Renata called me just as I was going out the front door.

"I've got to go to a meeting with my boss. Can't meet you for lunch and I'm so disappointed."

"Yeah, me too," I said. "So, when yuh wan'a get together again?"

"I really can't talk right now. I'll call you later."

"Okay," I said.

I felt like we were fading away from each other. We ended the conversation without setting up anything definite for the future. It felt like we were drifting apart. I was feeling like I might not see or hear from her again, kind of like last December when almost a month had passed, and we weren't in touch. I was hoping that it all wasn't slipping away, but I had an ominous feeling that it might be. I don't know why I was so insecure.

Days passed; I felt abandoned. Why wasn't she calling me? Why wasn't I calling her? Was this it, the end? I felt paralyzed. I couldn't answer any of these questions, much less act on them. I lied to myself, saying Debra still loved me and I still loved her, but I was sure it wasn't true. That relationship's days were num-bered.

Then one day after two weeks of silence, Renata called. I wasn't expecting it. In fact, I really wasn't ex-pecting her to call ever again. I was so happy to hear her

107

voice. She'd been in my head the whole two weeks. I managed to keep her there even though I was busy working on my three investigations.

She called to tell me that she, Bill and Tess were leaving in a couple days to visit her parents in Arizona. I froze at the thought of her going to Arizona. The feeling was reinforced with her next remark.

"We'll both be looking at the job and housing situations while we're there," she said.

"Oo. That mean you'll be moving soon?"

"I wouldn't say that. This is more of a scouting trip. Just the weekend. Driving down Friday, coming home Monday. We'll only be looking around."

"Guess yuh really can't do much on Saturday and Sunday."

"This is true. Don't worry. We won't be moving anytime soon."

"That's a relief."

"I'd like to see you again. Wan'a meet for lunch when I get back?"

"Absolutely!" I replied with maybe a little too much enthusiasm, but I couldn't help it.

"How 'bout next Wednesday, week from today?"

"Tell me when and where."

"Can you meet me at my office?"

"I can meet you anywhere you say. Your office is better. Won't have to go all the way into downtown. Get off the bus sooner."

"Good. My lunch hour starts at one o'clock."

Got no Secrets to Conceal

"I'll see yuh at a little before one next Wednesday."

"Can hardly wait."

"Me too."

"Hugs and kisses."

"'Bye."

So, it wasn't over! I'd see her in a week, and we'd pick up where we left off. I was happy again, but I was still unsure how it was going to go next Wednesday and after.

Friday came and my thoughts of her became very intense. I imagined her sitting in the car next to her spouse with their daughter in the back seat, and then I felt like I myself was on the road again, this time to Arizona instead of Reno. I thought about her constantly over the weekend, hoping that their journey would be safe, and suddenly fearing that it might not be, and I might never see her again. Then I put this fear out of my mind, and before I knew it, Tuesday arrived and she was talking to me on the phone, confirming our date for the next day. I couldn't describe how happy I was to hear her voice again. Now, after three weeks, I'd be seeing her the next day.

"So, how was your trip?" I asked when we were seated at a little restaurant in Freedom called the Wooden Nickel Too.

"Fine. Bill's flying back there in June. While we were there, he talked to a company on the phone, and he set up an interview with them on Monday the sixteenth. I'll be driving him to the airport on Friday the thirteenth."

109

"'Sounds like bad news to me. You may be moving to Arizona sooner than you thought."

"Oh, I don't know about that. It's only an interview, you know. I do have some good news. Wan'a hear it?"

"Please. I could use some good news."

"That's the same weekend as my graduation, and I thought I'd go to the ceremony. It's on Saturday at noon. Maybe I could come by your place. Spend the afternoon with you."

"'Sounds like a good plan, but what about Tess? You got a sitter? And yuh know I've got to be thinking about Debra here. She might wan'a do something, or she could just pop in on me unannounced. That wouldn't be pretty at all."

"Bill's taking Tess with him on the plane. My parents'll look after her while he's interviewing. They'll be happy to have her again for a couple days. Don't know what to say about Debra. Since Bill will be gone, maybe we could meet at my place after the ceremony."

"Now that sounds like a plan."

We finished our lunch and went back to her office where we hugged and then I walked the one block to the bus stop at the shopping center.

Sixteen

Spring was coming to an end; the long, warm days of summer were just around the corner. Plans for Renata's graduation weekend were all worked out. A week after that lunch date, Debra told me she planned a weekend trip with her friend Carol to Point Lobos. It was more of an in-service weekend than a pleasure trip. They'd be staying at Asilomar, a conference center on the Seventeen Mile Drive. They'd signed up for a class that explored the tide pools at Point Lobos. Debra and Carol, who was also a teacher, would get credit for the class, and the credit counted toward their cumulative units, which would move them up on the pay scale.

As soon as I found out about it, I called Renata to tell her the good news. We set up another lunch date so that we could talk about it in more detail. I took another bus ride out to Watsonville and got off at Crestview Shopping Center again. I got there at about twenty to one, so I had plenty of time before her lunch hour started. I walked over to her office and found a place on the lawn of the county courthouse annex and read my book. My heart jumped when I looked up from my reading and saw her walking toward me. It had been a couple weeks since I'd seen her, and she looked so good that I was instantly aroused. I stood up as she approached, and we hugged, but didn't kiss, as we came together. I hung onto the hug after she relaxed from it.

Jerome Arthur

"Where yuh wan'a eat?" I asked, still hugging her.

"How about the pizza place in the shopping center. They've got a salad bar and other things besides pizza."

"'T's go."

We walked across the street and through the shopping center to the restaurant at the other end. She got a salad from the salad bar and I got a turkey sandwich. She said the sautéed mushrooms were good, so we ordered some to share.

"So, wha'da yuh think about this mountain blowing its top?" she asked. She was referring to Mount Saint Helens, which had erupted just four days earlier. "Some of the pictures they showed on television were pretty wild, but you wouldn't know about that, would you?"

She was referring to the fact that I didn't have a television set. When I wanted to watch T.V., I'd go up to Debra's, and that was only when she invited me because she wanted me to see something she thought I'd like.

"I saw something about it in the paper, but I really haven't followed it. Probably go'n'a screw up the weather this summer."

"No doubt. You should've seen the pictures on television. Smoke and molten rock spewing out of it. It was really something."

Then we changed the subject and talked about her graduation weekend.

Got no Secrets to Conceal

"So, here's the deal for the weekend of the four-teenth," I said. "Debra's gone for both days. We can meet at my place after the graduation."

"Great!"

"What time you go'n'a be done?"

"The ceremony starts at eleven. I should be able to make it to your place by two."

"Cool. Think you can spend the night."

"Glad you suggested it. Done."

"Hey, let's plan on it."

"I'll be there!"

She sounded so sexy. It was a "...come-up-and-see-me-sometime..." moment for me. Then her two-toned eyes flashed flinty as she changed the subject.

"Bill's been a real shit, lately. I think the inter-view's making him nervous."

"So, what's the deal?"

"It's a well-established electronics company that recently moved its operation from over the hill to Phoe-nix. I don't know what he's worried about. He's got an application in at Shugart in Scotts Valley as well. I just wish he'd stop brooding. He's even had a couple of tem-per tantrums. It's unlike him to be that way. He's one of the most gentle, nonviolent people I've ever known. I don't know what's gotten into him. I think he might be threatened because I have a job and he's not going to have one."

"Did he quit his job?"

"Oh, yes. Didn't I tell you? He gave notice when we came back from Prescott. Next week is his last week. He couldn't stand seeing Tess going to daycare. He'll

113

get her into a co-op nursery school when he starts being with her every day. He's already talking to one in Ben Lomond. He'll volunteer at the school a couple days a week. Didn't I tell you he wanted to be a househusband?"

"You sure did. So that's it, huh? Finally got his wish."

"That's it. I just wish he'd get it worked out, and I think he will once he settles in with Tess and gets this interview over with. Says he's worried about the money."

"Maybe he knows you're out screwin' around and it's botherin' 'im."

"I doubt that. He's not the jealous type. That kind of thing doesn't bother him. Doesn't seem to care about it." The more I heard this line, the more I thought she was only trying to convince herself. "All I know is he'd better snap out of it pretty soon because I won't stick around and get dragged down by it."

"'Sounds like it's been going on a while."

"Only since I went back to work. What's that, a couple of months?"

We finished our lunch and went for a walk through the cemetery across the street. Nobody was there, so we were able to hug and kiss as much as we liked. Even though she said she didn't care if anybody saw her kissing someone who wasn't her husband, she still was somewhat discreet in public, but not here in the cemetery. We stayed in each other's embrace for the last ten minutes of her lunch hour. I had difficulty pulling myself away, but I had to, because she had to go back to

114

Got no Secrets to Conceal

work, and I had an appointment at one of the insurance companies I was working for. We walked back to her office, hugged one more time, and I went to the shopping center to catch my bus.

Seventeen

Suddenly I was feeling good about our relationship again. In a way I was glad she was having trouble with Bill. Somehow, I took that to mean she was more interested in me than she was in him.

Over the next three weeks, we talked twice a day, three or four days a week, right up to the big weekend. I felt myself being drawn in deeper and deeper, and I liked it, and I sensed that she liked it, too. I was falling in love.

We set up another lunch date on Monday the ninth and met again at the Wooden Nickel Too. After the waitress took our order, we talked about the upcoming weekend.

"Hope I can rise to the occasion," I said.

"You've never had any trouble in the past, not with me anyway," she replied in her sexy, smoky voice.

"This'll be the first time we'll spend the night together. How long we been doing this now? Six months? And we haven't spent a whole night together yet. I can't wait."

"Me too," she said, and then we just stared at each other, lost in each other's gaze.

The waitress broke the spell by setting our order down on the table.

"Leticia's starting to resent taking orders from me," she said.

"Really? What's that about."

Got no Secrets to Conceal

"I'm not sure. She isn't rebelling outright, but she's forgetting, quote/unquote, to do some of the small things I ask her to do, and I'm sure she's doing it on purpose. She's acting like she should be giving me orders because she's been there longer than I, even though I'm her supervisor rather than the other way around. Looks like I'll have to talk to her if she doesn't straighten up, because my boss is starting to question me on some of these things. We've just got to get the work done and not be involving ourselves in petty disputes about who's been there the longest and who should be taking orders from whom."

I noticed a hard edge in her tone as she spoke, and her obsidian pupils flashed like black crystal in her green and amber eyes. It was the second time I'd seen this in as many weeks. She looked like that at our last lunch date when she was talking about Bill's attitude. It was almost as if she were steeling herself against some inevitable reality, making herself strong so that if anybody was going to be hurt, it wouldn't be her. I was quickly learning that this was her defense mechanism, her means of surviving some of the cruel realities of human relationships. This part of her personality puzzled me. I wondered why she couldn't relax and just once be vulnerable. She must have opened herself at one time and had been hurt so badly that she was determined never to let it happen again. Maybe it was that guy she said she'd cared for a lot and didn't tell him. Her ex-boss, I had come to learn. But it seemed to go beyond mere self defense, rather it seemed to be an offensive tactic. Not

117

only was she not going to be hurt, she was going to hurt anybody who might get in her way.

We finished our lunch, paid the bill and went out to her car. Back at her office, we hugged and kissed, and I caught my bus back to Santa Cruz.

"I sure had a good time today," I said when I called her just as soon as I got back to my office.

"Likewise. You take care now and I can't wait for Saturday. I hope we can talk on the telephone between now and then."

"Absolutely! I'll call you tomorrow morning. Talk to you then."

"'Bye."

And the connection was broken, but we spoke to each other by phone twice a day right up to Saturday. I'd call her in the morning, and she'd call me in the afternoon.

"I sure hope nobody's checking these calls I'm making," she said on her Wednesday afternoon call to me.

"Me too."

Her concern was genuine. Calls between Watsonville and Santa Cruz were long distance, and I noticed that my phone bill was higher than usual during the last two months. Apparently nothing ever came of it on her end. I was the only one who had to answer for my bill, and I didn't mind spending the extra money because I liked to talk to her. The phone calls made the time pass.

So now it seemed that everything was coming together at once. I was having this beautiful love affair with Renata. I was feeling that my life was perfect, so

118

Got no Secrets to Conceal

perfect in fact that I was no longer concerned with rec-
onciling myself to my relationship with Debra. She was
just there. She hadn't told me so, but I was sure that Renata was just as contented with the relationship as I was.
I could sense it in my conversations with her, and since
she was calling me as much as I was calling her, I figured that she must be as taken with me as I was with her.
I wondered if I would be satisfied to see her only occasionally, yet I wasn't expecting her to leave Bill to spend
more time with me. She hadn't given me any indication
that she might do it, and when I thought about it, I hadn't
considered leaving Debra for her. I was thinking about
Renata being with me in the distant future, but I didn't
know how all this figured in the present situation, and
then I didn't know what Renata's feelings about this
were.

Eighteen

By Friday my anticipation of the weekend was overpowering me. I was so flush with expectation that it was almost like being drugged. At times I was confused, albeit in a good way, confusion from excitement that ultimately would make things crystal clear, or so I thought at the time. The two of us would think we were so clear on that weekend that we could only marvel at it. All our communication would come into sharp focus, and we'd be bright and lucid in the center of the nimbus that enveloped us.

I stayed busy through the morning, which helped relieve some of the anxiety of anticipating the next day. I took a break at noon, got on my bike and rode out to the Lane to check out the waves. On my way I picked up a couple of chile verde burritos from Las Palmas Taco Bar. I sat on a bench at Indicators and ate my burritos. It was a medium tide, and because of the sandbar that had built up all the way from Middle Peak to Outside Cowell's, some nice sets were coming through. There were a lot of people in the water. It was such a beautiful day and the sets were there, so I decided to get a session in.

I finished my burritos and peddled back to the cottage. It took me about ten minutes to get ready, and I was in the water by one-thirty. I got a lot of good rides at Indicators, even got one from Outside Cowell's all the

Got no Secrets to Conceal

way to the beach. My legs were tiring by the time I got there, but I held onto it. I stayed on the shoulder and skimmed along. I finally kicked out just before the wave turned to white water. I was so close to the beach that the water was only knee-deep, so I walked out of the surf and headed over to the steps. I went up to the bike path and carried my board down to Indicators where my bike was locked to the railing at the Point.

When I got back to the cottage, I took a shower and started getting the place ready for tomorrow. I couldn't do too much because Debra was coming by and we were going to dinner at China Schezuan a block behind my place on Cathcart Street. I had to hide the bottle of The Glenlivet I'd bought for Renata to celebrate her graduation with a shot of scotch. I had beer in the refrigerator for myself, but I didn't have to hide it because Debra was used to me having beer around, but not something as exotic as The Glenlivet Scotch.

"What time you taking off tomorrow?" I asked as we ate our mu shu pork with four pancakes and sweet and sour shrimp.

"About ten. We'll spend the morning getting checked into Asilomar, have some lunch and go to the first class at one-thirty. What'll you be doing?"

"Surf was great today. I'll pro'bly go out again tomorrow."

I hoped the lie wasn't showing on my face. A bolt of guilt shot through me, but I dismissed it quickly when I thought about Renata and the afternoon and evening we were going to have together.

121

"Want me to spend the night?" she asked. "I'll have to leave early so I can get ready to meet Carol by ten."

"Sure," I said. "Let's go over to Warehouse Liquors when we leave here. Pick up some wine for a nightcap. It'll be fun. Been a while since we spent the night together."

We finished our dinner and went to the liquor store. When we got back to my place, I put some Billy Holiday on the record player, and we had some wine and made love. It was the best love-making Debra and I ever had. She was so caring and considerate. Creative too. I was falling in love with her again. I wondered what was going on. My first thought was that she'd maybe seen the lust in Renata's flinty eyes that day in the Oak Room.

As I expected, Debra was out the door by eight o'clock. I looked at my tide chart and saw that low tide was about two hours away, so I got on my bike and went to look at Indicators again. The swell was picking up and guys were carrying their boards down the steps to the water. I peddled back home and got my board and was in the water by nine-thirty.

Nineteen

Renata's graduation ceremony was at eleven o'clock. She told me she'd try to make it to my place by two. I got out of the water at noon after a good two-hour session. I showered out back and was ready and waiting for her by one-fifteen. I sat down at my desk and worked on the file of one of my insurance cases. My phone rang at a quarter to two.

"Hi. I might be a little late," Renata said over dance music blasting in the background. "Can you hear the music?"

"How could I not? It's pretty loud."

"I just couldn't resist getting in a couple dances! They're having a party here at Kresge!"

"Oh," I said, disappointment registering clearly in my voice.

She must have sensed it as she said,

"Okay, I'll come right down."

"Oh, cool. See yuh when yuh get here."

I'd left the front door unlocked so all she had to do when she got there was walk in. I was working in my office when I heard it open. I called to her to lock it behind her. She came through the entry and into my small living room. I stood up and met her there. She looked a little tired from everything she'd been doing that morning. I embraced her and held onto her for a little longer than was necessary.

"Wan'a drink? I got a fifth a' Glenlivet just for you."

"Oh, how sweet. Yes, I'll have a shot. On the rocks, please."

I poured her a shot of scotch and opened a beer for me. We sat down and toasted her graduation and relaxed with our drinks.

"How was it?" I asked.

"I didn't even go through the ceremony. They had it at the Quarry Amphitheater, and I just stayed at the back and watched the other graduates get their degrees."

"Really? Yuh didn't even go up on stage?"

"I *did* go to the party after."

"So I heard."

After a while she said she wanted to take a shower. I gave her a beach towel and she started to undress. I sat down on the floor and watched her.

"I get hot just watching you."

"Should I do a performance for you?"

"Not necessary. I just like to watch you undress the way you do it naturally."

When her panties fell to the floor, she picked up the beach towel she'd draped over the chair and wrapped it around her middle. Then she went into the bathroom, took a bath towel off the rack and tossed it over her bare shoulder. She went out the back door to the shower. Fifteen minutes later she came back in, her slim torso still concealed by the beach towel, her long hair swathed in the bath towel. She was trying as best she could to get the ends of her long hair dry with the smaller towel.

Got no Secrets to Conceal

While she was showering, I got the bed turned down and took everything off but my boxer shorts. When she got her ends to the point where they were just damp, not dripping, she let the beach towel drop at almost the same time as my shorts hit the floor. We kissed and caressed standing next to the bed.

"I wan'a taste you," she said dropping to her knees.

She got me hard, and we slipped into bed and made love, strong and slow. We stayed in bed for a couple hours, making love until we were both spent.

"Wan'a go for a walk? Maybe go down to West Cliff?"

"Might be kinda' nice."

"Okay let's get outa' bed and get dressed."

"Ah, do we have to?" she said languorously.

"Well, maybe not right away."

We made love one more time before we got up.

We got out of bed relaxed and slow. It seemed to take us forever to get dressed. It was still light out when we got out of the house, but the sun was sinking fast. The first day of summer was one week off. We walked arm in arm, not worrying about being seen by anybody we knew. Another dumb thing I did in the affair. We went to the end of the wharf and then out to Cowell's. When we got to Lighthouse Point, the sun was just reaching the western horizon.

"Wow, just in time for the sunset. Too bad we don't get to see it go down over the water. Wrong time a' year. October to March. We should come out here tomorrow morning at sunrise. Should be pretty good if it's not foggy. This time a' year, sun comes up over the Salinas Valley. Looks like it's coming up over the Bay. Beautiful!"

"You've really studied it, huh? Think we can get up that early?"

"Yeah. I'm usually up before sunrise anyway."

"Me too. When you have a two-year-old scrambling around at six and you have to be to work at eight, believe me, you're up before the sun."

"No doubt. I guess we ought'a be outa' the house by at least six if we wan'a be in time for it. We'll have plenty a' time to make it up to the Chancellor's brunch. We still doin' that?"

"Definitely."

When we got back to my place, we slipped out of our clothes. She hadn't put on any underwear, so when her pants and blouse came off, she was completely naked. We fell into each other's arms, dropping into bed where we made furious love for another hour before falling into a deep sleep.

"You mind being awakened in the middle a' the night for more love making?" I asked.

"Not at all...."

She was sound asleep.

The point was moot, as was the possibility of watching the sunrise in the morning, because we both slept soundly until almost seven o'clock, at which time we made crazy love again. We showered together and made love one more time with wild abandon before we sat down and had something to eat. We barely finished breakfast and we were at it again. At a quarter to ten, we

126

Got no Secrets to Conceal

finally got out of the house and headed up to the U. in her car.

The brunch reception at the Chancellor's residence for all the graduates of the past two days started at eleven. She parked on a residential street outside the university entrance, and we walked over to the bus stop. It was a beautiful morning, and as we waited for a bus to come, we basked in the warm sun.

"We could try to hitch a ride," she said.

"I'll pass on that," I said. "Besides its being dangerous, there are certain people I wouldn't want to see me hitchhiking."

"It is dangerous, it's true," she said. "I've only done it once, and that was on campus. One day I was late for a class, so I hitched across campus, and it was strange doing it. I was nervous the whole time I was in the car. Breathed a sigh of relief when the guy let me off."

"I used to hitchhike all the time when I was a teenager, but things were a lot different in those days. I don't think it was so dangerous back then. I just don't do it anymore."

A bus rumbled up and we got on. Within minutes we were at the Chancellor's house. He greeted everybody at the front door, and I shook his hand as I introduced myself. When we got inside, we helped ourselves to the abundance of fresh fruit, Danish, coffee and orange juice. I saw a friend who'd just completed his doctorate. His wife, a friend of Debra's, was with him. Suddenly I was feeling uneasy, wondering if this would get back to her. Renata was aware of my tension and asked me if I wanted to be leaving soon.

"It might not be a bad idea," I said, "but I don't wan'a take you away from your party. This will be the second time in two days."

"Oh, it's all right. I just wanted to make an appearance here. I should be getting back to my house anyway. Want to come up and spend the afternoon with me?"

"Yeah. How yuh wan'a do it? Want me to follow you in my car?"

"Sure."

It was getting on to noon, so we slipped out the door unnoticed. I suggested we walk back down to her car rather than wait for a bus. The entrance to the bike path was right next to the Chancellor's house, and that's the route we took. There was no traffic there, and some of the views of Monterey Bay were breathtaking. As we walked down the bike path, I explained to Renata who my acquaintances at the brunch were.

"Main thing I'm worried about is whether the woman's go'n'a tell Debra that she saw me there with you."

"No use worrying about it now. You'll just have to wait and see."

As we walked down the hill, ground squirrels popped out of their holes, scurrying across the bike path and finding other holes to pop into. We stopped a couple times and hugged and kissed. We walked arm-in-arm down the bike path. We got back to Renata's car by twelve-thirty.

Got no Secrets to Conceal

She was hurrying so that we could have as much time together as possible. We rode the rest of the way down off the hill sighing. She pulled over in front of my bungalow, and I got out. I didn't even go in the house. Instead, I walked down the driveway to the garage and got my car out.

I got behind her and followed her up the hill. So far, the weekend was perfect. We were completely consumed with each other. We made love in her waterbed, a first for me. We took a walk in the woods. I'm not a religious man, but I've decided that if there is such a thing as heaven, I must've been there that weekend. I was sure that I was hopelessly, irrevocably in love with her, and I hoped she felt the same way about me. On the walk in the redwoods, she told me she never felt clearer than she did right then. We were aglow with the love that consumed us. The electricity that crackled between us sparkled in our imaginations. Again, we returned to her waterbed and made intense, feverish love and then fell into a deep sleep. We awoke at six o'clock.

"I probably should be going," I said. "Don't you have to start getting ready for work tomorrow?"

"Yes, I do."

We hugged and kissed fervently. This was the most difficult moment. We couldn't seem to tear ourselves away from each other, but we had to, so we did. I got dressed and got ready to leave. Thus was ending the much anticipated weekend, but it wasn't quite over. Bill wasn't due to come home for two more days, and that gave us a few more opportunities to get together.

When I got home, there was a message from Debra on my answering machine.

"Wan'a come up for dinner?" she asked. "Call me."

I called her back.

"It's not too late, is it?" I asked when she picked up.

"Not at all. Come on up."

"I've got a couple things to do and then I'll drive right up."

I spent a few minutes straightening up the cottage so that there weren't any remnants of my weekend of lust and love with Renata for Debra to pick up on. I threw in a load of laundry, and then I called Renata. We talked for about ten minutes, repeatedly telling each other how clear we felt and what a wonderful weekend we'd had together. Then I hung up and drove up to Debra's place.

I was feeling channeled in the same rut that I'd escaped over the last two days. I was suddenly feeling stifled like never before. For the first time in the seven years that I'd been with Debra, I was feeling like I didn't want to be with her anymore. I began to imagine how it would be to be with Renata and how I could get away from Debra, but I couldn't figure how, especially without hurting her. The more I thought about the situation, the more impossible I realized it was. In the first place Renata had no intention of leaving Bill, at least not now. I remembered that she had once told me it was hard for her to imagine staying with him for the rest of her life, but then in the next breath, she told me she had a com-

mitment to see it through until Tess was raised. Realizing the impossibility of it all, I attempted to put it out of
my mind, thus settling back into the rut I knew I couldn't
escape.

Twenty

That weekend, which wasn't quite over, was just the beginning of a dizzying period that lasted two months. I had ambivalent feelings of clarity and confusion all at once. I remembered every episode; they went by so quickly. They came into sharp focus and then moved along and blurred. I was so high, savoring every moment, and when the moment passed on, I'd come down, feeling like I'd lost something, but my overall feeling was good. Something happened to me that I'd never experienced before in my life, and I wasn't sure I'd ever experience it again. All I knew was that I liked it.

Renata called me first thing Monday morning.

"You've got to find some way to get up to my place tonight," she blurted before I could say anything.

"Well hello to you, too, and good morning."

"I'm not sure I can make it through the day without seeing you."

"I'll make it up there. Not to worry. I wan'a see you as much as you wan'a see me."

We set a time, and once again, I was filled with anticipation. From that moment on, the day seemed to drag. Debra called me when she got home from work.

"Wha'da yuh say we go down to Riva's for dinner?"

"Whoa. I wasn't expecting that," I replied.

Got no Secrets to Conceal

"Well, do you want to, or not?"

She sounded a bit agitated.

"Uh, yeah, sure," I stammered. "But we got'a go early, 'cause Charles and I're goin' out to O.T.'s around nine." I hated to lie to her, but I just couldn't help myself. "Go'n'a have a couple beers and listen to the music."

"How 'bout six. That early enough for you?"

"Perfect."

I called Renata and told her I couldn't get up to see her until nine-thirty.

"Oh, my god! What'm I go'n'a do! I don't think I can wait that long!"

"I know, I know. It's go'n'a be hard for me too, but look at it this way. I'll stay all night, if you'll have me."

"Are you kidding? Once you come through my door, I'm not letting you out till tomorrow morning. You'll be my prisoner."

That was a good thought. I spent the rest of the afternoon doing paperwork. Debra pulled up in front of the bungalow, and I went out to greet her.

"Hey, how yuh doin'?" I said as I got into her car.

"You okay? You seem a little out of sorts."

"I'm okay. Just thinking how much I missed you when you were down in Monterey."

"Hmm."

That was all she said until we were looking at the view from the window at Riva, and then it was only to answer my question.

"So, how was the class?"

"Lota' fun. Explored the tide pools at Point Lobos. How was *your* weekend? You do anything worthwhile?"

"Not really," I said, trying not to sound too much like I was lying. "Went surfing Saturday. Stayed home Sunday. Went to the Coop in the afternoon for a bit. Listened to the band."

I was treading on dangerous ground here. I felt like a heel. I was still trying not to sound like a liar, but I wasn't even convincing myself.

"That's it, huh?" she said and then she shifted her gaze to the cliff and shoreline along Cowell's Beach.

"Pretty much." I didn't want to say more because I didn't want to get in more trouble than I already seemed to be in. I asked her more about her weekend. "Wha'd yuh learn about the tide pools at Point Lobos?"

"Not much more'n what I already knew about the tide pools out at Mitchell's Cove. Sea life is the same. Mollusks and anemones."

"Sounds cool."

We didn't talk much as we ate, not necessarily because we were too busy eating, but because there was tension between us. I had the feeling she knew there was something going on outside our relationship. My hunch was confirmed when she dropped me off at my place at around eight. When I leaned over to kiss her before she drove away, she gave me the cold shoulder. Maybe I was wrong, but I didn't think so at the time.

I didn't wait until nine to take off for Renata's house. I was so excited to see her for the third day in a

Got no Secrets to Conceal

row that I left my place almost as soon as Debra turned the corner at Walnut. I got into the car and drove straight up Highway Nine to her place in Boulder Creek. As I drove through this forest, I wondered how she could live in such a place. Right now, it was nice, but I could imagine how damp and dark it must get in the winter months. She opened her front door wearing a slinky floor length peignoir and invited me in.

A reel-to-reel tape player on the credenza next to the T.V. was playing Buffy Sainte-Marie's "The Universal Soldier" as I entered. When that song ended, Bob Dylan came on with "Watching the River Flow." We sat on the couch and talked and listened.

"Pretty nice setup you have there. I didn't notice it when I was here Saturday. 'Course, I wasn't noticing much of anything except you."

"All Bill. He's an audiophile. See the albums down below."

When I looked where she was pointing, I saw that the whole lower shelf on the credenza was filled with albums. He had fashioned shelves next to the credenza that were also filled with albums.

Gloria Gaynor came on, and Renata stood up and danced for me. I watched her and thought how beautiful she looked writhing to the music.

"I love dancing," she said. "It's like screwing, only standing up."

The song ended and she took me by the hand, and as I stood up, I drew her to me and gave her a long, deep kiss. Then we were off to her waterbed.

135

Jerome Arthur

"Wow, this is only the second time I've ever been in a waterbed," I said. "Sunday was the first."

"Virgin rushes are always the best," she said, and we were making wild love again.

"I love you," I said, before I realized the words were out.

I was afraid as soon as I uttered the words that it was the wrong thing to say. That's why I was surprised when she responded the way she did. It was exactly what she wanted to hear.

"Oh," she responded, "I love you too, a lot." As we lay spent, she snuggled close to me, caressing my chest with her long, smooth fingers. "We ought to go to Tahiti or some place like that after my kid grows up and leaves home. That sound like a good idea?"

"Are you serious?" I asked. "That sounds like a great idea! When do we leave?"

"Well, I want to wait till my kid grows up. Like maybe when she finishes high school?"

"I don't know if I can wait that long. Yuh know, Debra wants to get married. She's not go'n'a wait much longer."

"Well, wha'da yuh say? Wan'a go to Tahiti? We could lie on the beach and screw all day and night. Wouldn't that be wonderful?"

"Let's plan on it," I replied.

"You know, this could just be a great big infatuation," she said. "But I don't think it is. This is it! Isn't it? You're a hard person to be in lust with, so I think I'm just go'n'a have to be in love with you."

136

Got no Secrets to Conceal

"That's fine with me, 'cause I know I'm in love with you, and I can't help it. That's just the way it'll have to be."

"You also know that Bill and Tess are coming into the airport in San José on Wednesday night."

"Yes, I know. So how 'bout I come up again tomorrow night? One last time before you get back into your marriage routine."

"Yes, do!"

We fell back into some heavy lovemaking. We felt so close to each other, and we really loved each other and were in love too. The hours passed, and the time came that I had to be getting back home. At around five in the morning, I dragged myself out of her warm waterbed and into her warm shower. When I got my clothes on, it was that melancholy time again when lovers must separate until the next time. We hugged and kissed all the way out the front door. The door closed behind me and I was stepping high going down the hill to my car.

I turned the car radio on coming down off the mountain, Highway Nine to Graham Hill Road to Highway One. It was perfect. Sam Cook was singing "You Send Me."

Twenty-one

I got to her house at a little after seven Tuesday night. She opened the door before I could knock and stood in the open doorway with nothing on but a very sexy, diaphanous negligee. She grabbed me and pulled me in before I could say anything, and the next thing I knew, I was on my back on her living room floor, and she was taking me between her sweet lips and she did it like Linda Lovelace in *Deep Throat*. When she got me big and hard, she climbed on top and slammed away at me. And that's how it went throughout the night. I finally pulled myself away after midnight and drove home.

I was so lost in reverie that I missed the turn at Graham Hill Road and ended up going down Highway Nine to get home. Renata was all I could see. I couldn't get her out of my head, and she was talking like she couldn't get me out of hers. That Tuesday night we expressed mutual anxiety about having to wait another sixteen years before we could be "together permanently." We wondered together if we could endure staying with our respective mates until that time, and I wasn't even married to mine yet. I was already thinking how my life would be without Debra. For her part Renata said she probably wouldn't be able to stay with Bill for too long if I broke off my engagement, knowing that I was "out there," as she put it. I could've sworn I detected a note of jealousy in her tone, and I liked the feeling. It was the

Got no Secrets to Conceal

same feeling I got the night she dropped me at the Oak Room after we'd spent the evening at the Casa Blanca. I couldn't describe the look on her face, then or now, except to quote Eric Clapton singing, "I feel wonderful each time I see the love light in your eyes/and the wonder of it all that you just don't realize/how much I love you."

"Wonder." That's the word. Like "the wonder of it all." I wondered if it was all real, if it was really happening to me.

When I got home, I saw that there were two messages on my answering machine. They were both from Debra. The first one was left at eight o'clock.

"Hi, honey. Guess you went out for a beer or something. Call me when you get home. I really would like to see you tonight. Maybe you could come up. Spend the night. Let me know if you want to. Talk to you later." The second call came in at nine o'clock. "Hi honey. Where are you?" She sounded irritated. "I'm going to bed now, so you don't have to come up. Maybe tomorrow night."

I looked at the clock. It was almost one a.m. Too late to call now and definitely too late to go up there. Her tone worried me. She sounded troubled. I wondered if she'd caught on to me and Renata. I brushed my teeth and went to bed.

Bill and Tess weren't getting in until later in the evening on Wednesday, and Renata wanted to see me once more before they got home.

"I'm going to Ramona's after work today," she said when she called in the morning. "I've got'a see you

139

once more before my spouse and kid get home. They won't be coming in till nine o'clock, so there's time, and our chances after they get here'll be slim."

"What time and where?"

"How 'bout the beach in front of the Casa Blanca at six-thirty?"

"'Sounds like a plan. See yuh there."

I was busy all day doing paperwork on the three insurance cases, and Rob Novak called me about tracking down a woman's daughter who hadn't been brought home from her weekend visitation with her father, the woman's ex-husband.

Debra called in the afternoon.

"Can you come up tonight? I'll fix you dinner, and maybe you can spend the night."

"Boy, does that ever sound good, but I can't come for dinner. Can't get there till maybe eight." I was thinking maybe an hour with Renata. "I just picked up a job from Rob Novak today, and I'm go'n'a meet 'im at six-thirty. He's got a client wants me to find her daughter. Ex didn't bring her home from weekend visitation." I was lying through my teeth about the meeting with Rob and hoped it didn't sound like it. I wasn't really lying about the case because that part of it was true.

"Ookay. I'll see yuh at eight."

She sounded skeptical.

"I'll try to make it earlier if I finish my meeting sooner."

I left the house at six-fifteen and walked down to the beach. School was out and so were the crowds at the beach. I was leaning up against the iron rail fence as she

Got no Secrets to Conceal

emerged from that small crowd on my right. We walked to Cowell's Beach, which was less crowded than Main Beach. We crossed the beach to the cliff next to the Dream Inn. We found a small outcrop of cliff where we couldn't be seen by anybody on the beach, and we kissed passionately. Suddenly we were in a different place. The beach could have been crowded or not. I didn't care. We were so lost in each other.

The sun had gone behind the cliff above us before we got there. A good piece of the beach and surf were still in sunshine. There was a slight breeze. The longest day of the year was three days off. We were the only people near the cliff. There were two kids playing in the high tide. Their family and a couple of others were still in sunshine. They looked like they were ready to pack up and leave. There were no surfers in the water.

"Bill and Tess will be landing at eight o'clock tonight," she said. She was clearly disappointed at the prospect. "I miss my kid, and it'll be nice to have her home, but I don't know about my spouse. If he's not going to be nice, I don't want him around. Oh well, we'll see. How many years before we go to Tahiti?"

"Sixteen. Tess is coming up on, what, two? Got'a figure when she's eighteen, she should be outa' high school."

"Seems like such a long time," she said, and that faraway gaze flashed across her face. I hadn't seen it for a while. "Is this really happening to us, Jack? It seems like there's no getting away from it, is there?" Her tone was soft and affectionate.

"God, I love you," I said and hugged her again.

"I love you too."

We stayed for a while longer on the beach, and pretty soon she had to go. She'd said Bill and Tess were landing at eight, and he was parked in long term parking, so she thought they'd be home by nine. She wanted to be there before them, and since it was now moving toward seven-thirty, we were getting ready to split up. We stood up and hugged and kissed one more time.

Then we turned and headed back to Beach Street. She looped her arm through mine and snuggled up close to my shoulder. I felt like a lucky man to have such a beautiful lady in love with me. We split up at the Wharf. She went back to Ramona's and I went to my place. I was taking a shower by seven thirty-five and in the car on my way to Debra's by ten to eight. The phone rang as I was going out the door.

"I'm still at Ramona's," her voice spoke into the receiver. "I just wanted to say that I love you."

"I love you too," I said. "I knew you'd call. I could feel your presence. I sensed you were thinking about me. I'm on my way up to spend the night with Debra. I'll call you tomorrow morning."

"Good. I can hardly wait."

She hung up. I was feeling satisfied and proud. I imagined her in her car, me sitting beside her. We were on a highway going away. I got to Debra's house by five after eight.

"How'd your meeting go?" she asked.

"Not bad. It's not go'n'a be too tough a case."

"What kind of case is it?"

142

Got no Secrets to Conceal

"Woman trying to get her daughter back from her ex. She had custody; he had reasonable visitation rights. He picked the girl up one Friday night and didn't bring her back on Sunday. Like I say I got the job from Rob Novak. Three of us met at six-thirty at Rob's office. He's found out the guy's in town right now. Wants me to find him."

"You have anything to go on?"

"He gave me a couple leads. I'll get busy on 'em tomorrow."

"How long's the dad had the kid."

"Couple months."

"How old is she?"

"Little girl. Preschool age."

"Whatever's happening in her head can't be good. Two months away from mommy, she must be scared, even if her daddy is treating her well."

"I guess," I said. "So, you sounded a little irritated in the phone messages you left last night. Everything okay?"

"So so. Talked to my mom on the phone yesterday. Had an argument with her. And then I really wanted to see you, and you weren't home. Where were you?"

"Charles and I went out again. Just out carousing. Bending our elbows. Hit a couple joints."

I knew I was go'n'a have to come clean with her soon. I was feeling really guilty, all the lying. We finished our wine and went off to her bedroom. We had a really great night in bed, which was giving me second thoughts about leaving her for Renata.

143

Twenty-two

After that weekend, Renata and I talked twice a day by telephone on the weekdays, and on weekends she'd call me from Ramona's house on Saturday afternoon and from her own house on Sunday morning when Bill left to pick up the Sunday newspaper. He was looking for a job back in San José. The Arizona interview hadn't been encouraging. He still hadn't heard anything about the job after he'd been home two weeks. The best thing to come out of the trip, according to Renata, was that he and Tess had had a really good time together visiting the grandparents.

"He's been in better spirits since he got back," she said when she called Sunday morning. "Hope it lasts."

I could hear Tess gurgling and chattering in the background. Every once in a while, Renata would interrupt our conversation to say something to her.

"'Sounds like you're happy your daughter's home," I said.

"I did miss her, and yes, I'm glad she's back."

"Glad you could find time to call *me*. Won't be too long you won't be able to 'cause Tess'll be able to figure out you're talking to your lover. Yuh know, I sure love you."

"Likewise," she said.

Got no Secrets to Conceal

"See? Right there. How're you go'n'a explain stuff like 'likewise' to her when she gets old enough to ask?"

"Who knows, by that time I might not have to explain anything," she replied off-handedly. "I've got'a go now. Bill will be coming back any minute."

"Okay. Have a nice day. We'll talk tomorrow. I love you."

"Likewise," she said and was off the line.

She called first thing the next morning.

"I've got some things I need to do at Ramona's tonight. Things I didn't finish doing on Saturday. Wan'a meet me there at around eight o'clock? We could go down to the beach again."

"I'll be there. What's her address? Never been to her house."

She gave me the address and said she couldn't wait to see me again.

The day slipped by, and at about twenty to eight that evening, I left the house, heading toward Beach Hill. When I got to Ramona's, I thought the eugenia hedge surrounding it was kind of imposing. It seemed to say that whoever was behind it must certainly be hiding from something or someone, and when Renata introduced me to Ramona, I could see it was true. She was hiding from herself, watching television in a darkened parlor adjacent to the living room. She wore dark baggy clothes that covered every part of her except her neck and face. Her white lace gloves and her pale face were the only light-colored things on her. She was a red head. She acted very dreamy as though she were drugged, which she probably was. Renata had said that one of her problems was that she abused cocaine and diet pills. She didn't talk to me much, except to say, "how do you do," and then she gave Renata some instructions on something she wanted done with one of her checkbooks. When she finished telling her, she leaned forward on her couch, beckoning Renata to come over and hug her.

"You've been so wonderful to me," she told Renata as she hugged her. "I don't know how I would ever have made it without your help and support. Thank you, Renata. I love you."

"You just rest and take care of yourself," Renata replied. "I love you too."

When we were out of the house and on our way down to the beach, I said, "Looks like she had a rough night."

"She looks like that all the time. Shouldn't be mixing her drugs with alcohol. Really an addictive personality. She should quit altogether."

"The way she's all closed up inside that house reminds me of Norma Desmond in *Sunset Boulevard*."

"It may appear that she's alone, but she has a lot of traffic going through that house. It's not as though she's a recluse or anything like that, but that's not to say she's not lonely. Has lots of friends, but most of them are questionable. I've met a few when I've been working. They help her snort the cocaine she pays for. They're hanging around for a free ride. Bunch of creeps."

We walked in silence for a while, and when we got to Beach Street, she took her shoes off and put on

146

Got no Secrets to Conceal

some knee-high socks that Ramona had loaned her for walking on the beach. The weather had taken a turn for the worse as a light rain began to fall, but it wasn't cold, so it was a comfortable rain. We walked along the wet sand beside the Casino, and then up the stairs and onto the crowded Boardwalk. She put her shoes back on and we walked the length of the Boardwalk. Then we came back down onto Beach Street and started back toward the wharf. During this whole time, we talked about how much we loved each other and how nice it was going to be when we would leave our partners and go to Tahiti. When we came abreast of the Casa Blanca Inn, we both looked up the stairs and sighed, almost simultaneously.

"Should we get our room?" I asked. "It'll just take a minute to get registered."

"I don't think so," she replied. "There's nothing I'd like better, but I'll have to be getting home pretty soon."

When we got to Front Street, we went into Positively Front Street for beers. It was crowded, just like the Boardwalk and Beach Street. It was summer. We blended in and relaxed with our beers.

It was nine o'clock when we left the bar and headed back to Ramona's. We sat in Renata's car for a few minutes and talked and hugged and kissed. Like teenagers. At one point, Renata suggested that we go to the back bedroom in Ramona's house, but then she nixed that idea quickly for the same reason she didn't want to get a room at Casa Blanca. It was almost nine-thirty by that time, so I gave her one more hug and kiss, got out of the car, and watched forlornly as she drove away.

Jerome Arthur

I turned and headed for Lulu Carpenter's to have another beer before going home. I walked down the stairs to Laurel Street Extension and thought how wonderful my life was. I loved her so much that at times I thought I would burst with happiness, and then when I considered that she loved me just as much, I thought of it as some kind of miracle. *How could all this be possible,* I thought. Walking up Pacific Avenue, I felt so mellow and fulfilled that even the street people in front of Lulu's, whose presence usually irritated me, even when they weren't scrounging for spare change, didn't bother me.

I ordered a shot of The Glenlivet and a bottle of Beck's and sipped on each alternately. I still had over half a glass of beer by the time the shot glass was empty, and I was starting to feel it. The beer I had at Positively Front Street started it all, and now I was high. There was nobody else in the bar. At that moment I felt like I was the only person in the world. The walk home in the warm misty night was absolutely wonderful. I fell asleep, aglow with anticipation for the sound of Renata's voice in the morning.

Over the next two weeks, we saw each other almost daily. One night we rented a cabin in a bungalow court in Felton called the Toll House. Another night we got together in my office. Good thing Debra didn't want to go out that night. On another night I drove up to her house when Bill took Tess to San José and stayed the night with friends.

We were falling deeper and deeper in love, and mutually agreeing that the deeper we fell, the clearer it

Got no Secrets to Conceal

became. I couldn't remember when time went by faster for me, and the whole time I was feeling more fantastic than I'd ever felt in my life. The last time I could recall feeling anywhere near this enchanted was when I was a teenager and in love for the first time, but that only came close, and as Renata herself had put it once when she was talking about her high school sweetheart, "Did that really count? I was so young then." She couldn't praise me enough for our night at the Toll House. She referred to it as the night I did my "naked savage" act with her. That night was especially a clear one. Hemingway had written about the lucidity of drunkenness, but I thought there could be nothing that could clear the windows of perception better than sex with plenty of love behind it. I had had some lucid moments while drunk, but never any that shone as bright as these times with Renata. I was beginning to realize that I'd never really known love before.

She came into Santa Cruz one day on county business. She'd called me in advance to see if I could meet her before she went back to Watsonville. She had to go to the county mental health facility, so I told her I'd meet her there and then we could go to De Laveaga Park, which was close by, and spend some time together. I met her at one-thirty, and we went in her car up to the park. We found a private place where we could talk and be close.

"Went dancing last night with Carol," she said after we got settled on a picnic bench.

"Oh? Where 'bouts?"

"The Albatross. Ever hear of it?"

"Oh yeah."

"Had a really good time," she said, "but I'd rather have been with you. How nice it would've been if you'd been there. I could've danced with you all night. As it was, I had to settle for a guy named Jeffrey. He was a nice enough guy, a good dancer for sure, but I thought about you while I danced with him. I gave him my work phone number, and he called today. Wants to have lunch with me sometime. I told him maybe one day next week, so he said he'll call back Monday."

I felt a pang of jealousy dart through me, and it must have shown on my face because she got right into it.

"Do I detect a little jealousy here?"

"Should I be? Jealous, that is."

"You don't have to be. I told the guy I was married, but I was really trying to put him off because of you."

I was feeling better, but I was still a little distracted by, what seemed to me, her casual attitude. I was the one she said she loved. I also had to remind myself that jealousy was a possessive thing, and I didn't want to be possessive, but I couldn't help wondering why she had to go out with the guy at all. She could have lunch with me instead. I tried to let it slide out of my mind. There was really nothing I could do anyway. She had told me that she liked to go out with different guys, and if that's what she wanted to do, then she'd do it. We talked for about a half-hour, and then she said she had to be getting back to Watsonville, so she dropped me off at the corner of Ocean and Water and drove off.

Twenty-three

On July ninth she called me first thing in the morning.

"I've got to see you today," she said

"What's up? You okay? You sound anxious." I waited for the axe to fall.

"I've been trying to tell you how I feel about you," she said, "and I somehow don't think I've been very successful. Well, last night I lay awake thinking about it, and I decided to write you a letter. That's why I want to see you, to hand you the letter in person. Plus, I miss your hugs and kisses."

"Whew. That's good news, and I was afraid it was go'n'a be bad. Where yuh wan'a meet, and when?"

"I love you, Jack Lefevre. How about in front of our favorite motel at six."

"I love you too, Mrs. Lowell."

I heard a sexy, quiet giggle before she hung up.

At a quarter to six I headed down to the beach. This time Renata was already there sitting on a bench across the street from the Casa Blanca Inn. I made my way through the crowd to her.

"Hey. How's it goin'?"

"Better, now that we're together," she replied, wrapping her arms around me and giving me a strong hug.

"Let's go over to Cowell's where there aren't so many people."

"Okay."

We held hands till we got there, and as soon as we got under the cover of the cliff, we hugged and kissed and caressed each other. When we sat down in the sand, she opened her purse and took out a piece of folded notebook paper and handed it to me.

"Should I read it right now, or do you want me to wait until I'm alone."

"By all means, read it now."

I unfolded the paper and read:

Mi cielito,   *Midnight July 8*

I'm writing to tell you how much I love you. It seems it's easier to put down on paper what I can't seem to tell you. I find myself saying, "I want—I want" followed only by your name. I've only once had similar feelings and that was when I was in high school, but be assured those feelings were only similar, not the same. For twelve years I have searched for love, and now here you are. This love is bigger than both of us, and sometimes when I think about it, it scares me. I hope we will be together always. I love you.

152

Got no Secrets to Conceal

The letter was unsigned, which hardly mattered, since it was written in her own handwriting, which I considered to be a signature in itself. I was overcome with joy at reading those simple lines. They certainly expressed my feelings precisely, and I told her so. Then we fell into a long hug, and we kissed hotly, and we both felt that we had reached the apex of our love. We knew it would be hard to fly much higher. As we embraced, we watched the surf break on the sandbar at Outside Cowell's and looked at Monterey in the distance. It was Saturday evening, and she was expected home after she finished her work for Ramona, so she had to be leaving after what seemed to me to be only a flash in time. She stood up breathing a heavy sigh, and it was no sigh of relief. If anything, it was a sigh of distress for having to part. We walked back over to Ramona's. Before she went into the house we hugged again, and then she was gone.

Twenty-four

Over the next two weeks we were together on five different occasions, and we talked daily on the telephone. We were acting like teenagers in love, and just when I thought I had it made, she threw me another curve.

"Jeffrey called me and asked me out to lunch," she said offhandedly.

"Who's Jeffrey?"

"Don't you remember? I danced with him that night at the Albatross."

"Oh, yeah. I remember. So, you go'n'a go out with 'im?"

"You're not jealous, are you?"

"A little."

"Not to worry. I'll turn him down if he wants an intimate relationship, which I'm sure he does. Don't all guys? I can't believe I'm doing this. I'm go'n'a use Bill as my excuse to not get involved, but you're really the one I want to be faithful to. I don't want anyone else but you. Can you understand that?"

"I'm not sure I understood anything you just said, but I'm glad you want to be faithful to me. It makes me feel good."

And I couldn't have felt better than I did right then, but I knew I must have felt at least equally as good on a lot of occasions over the past month and a half.

Got no Secrets to Conceal

"I don't think you can be so sure I'm go'n'a be the only one for you. Glad you think so. I just hope it's true because I don't want anybody but you, and that's a fact. I love you so much it scares me. It's uncharted territory for me. I've never felt this way about anyone before in my life."

"Me either," she said quickly. "That's why I know you're the only one."

I had no reason to doubt anything she said. I was feeling very good about us, and I reinforced myself by reading her letter whenever doubts entered my mind.

Debra planned a train trip for us to Santa Barbara the first weekend in August. She would be starting the new semester on Monday. We were both busy getting things organized for it, so we were seeing more of each other. I still managed to see Renata often through the rest of July. We had breakfast at Tapu's Breakfast Hut early one morning before she went to work. It was her idea. As it turned out it was only an excuse for her to see me, just as her calling me to tell me that she had to run an errand at the county building and asking me if I wanted to meet her there was also an excuse for us to get together.

As July came to an end, I took stock of the past two months and reckoned that they were the best two months of my life. It was the best summer I'd ever had. During the last week in July, we met one evening at Positively Front Street to have a beer together. We were seated at the bar when she told me about her dilemma.

"When I make love to Bill, you're the one I'm thinking about, and I feel guilty for being unfaithful to

155

you. I'm beginning to be a little confused here. Think I should be worried?"

"Well, yuh got'a be a sex partner to your husband. I'm sure he expects it, and it is go'n'a be sixteen years before we can really be together, so I guess we're just go'n'a have to screw up our courage and deal with these problems till then."

"And we can make it, can't we?"

"We don't have any other choice."

She was taking a short break from her work at Ramona's house, so we finished our beers, left the bar, and started back up the hill.

"I've got a lunch date with my ex-boss tomorrow," she said. "Says he's got business in Salinas and wants to stop in on me on his way through from Santa Clara. Haven't seen him in two and a half years, and all of a sudden he calls me and wants to take me to lunch."

My heart dropped. My first thought was that this was the same guy she'd told me about last fall. She'd been so taken with him and hadn't told him for a long time, and now here she was going out with him again. I also thought this must be the guy she told me she'd "screwed with the Dictaphone turned on." It was just one of the stories she told me when she bragged about her many sexual adventures. She hadn't been doing that lately, at least not since we'd expressed our love for each other. I began to wonder if she was going to start up again: talking about her sexual past, and getting intimately involved with other men and telling me about it. I had a sinking feeling that she was. I tried to put it out of my mind. I remembered telling myself this would be one

156

Got no Secrets to Conceal

of the things I'd have to tolerate if I was going to be in love with her. Again, I wondered how Bill coped with it. That was the real puzzle in my mind. I couldn't figure how Bill could stand by and watch her come home at eleven o'clock and sometimes midnight, vaguely smelling of sex. I couldn't handle it myself. I was sure I would be crazy with jealousy. I *was* crazy with jealousy. Renata had always insisted that it really didn't bother Bill, but I thought I knew better. In fact, I thought that the reason her marriage was on the rocks was because Bill was fed up with her infidelity, and generally tired of her never being home to relate to him and Tess in a family way.

When we got to Ramona's house, we hugged and kissed. I walked home with these thoughts weighing heavily upon me.

The last time we got together was five days before Debra and I left for Santa Barbara. She stopped by my bungalow on her way to Ramona's. I was hoping we could spend a couple of hours together, but it didn't quite work out that way. She could only hang with me for an hour. We got in lots of hugs and kisses and that's all. When it was time for her to go, we both regretted it. We had so much fun together, even without the sex, that memories of any negative thoughts from our last meeting went away. I was right back on track again, all satisfied and proud.

Twenty-five

On the Tuesday after Debra and I got home from Santa Barbara, as I was sitting at my desk working on the files for one of the insurance companies I was contracted to, there was a knock on the front door. I summoned the person to enter. A tall, dark, bearded guy came in. He approached me with his right hand extended.

"Hello, I'm Bill Lowell and I'd like to talk to you about retaining your services," he said. He was soft spoken.

I don't know if my shock showed at the mention of his name. I don't see how it couldn't.

"Uh, hello, I...I'm Jack Lefevre." I shook his hand. "Wh...who recommended me to you?"

"I found you in the yellow pages. Didn't wan'a call yuh on the phone, 'cause I wanted to talk to you in person."

Now, I was really starting to get nervous! More like panic. Was he on to Renata and me? No, that couldn't have been it. He said he wanted to hire me.

"What can I do for you?"

I was so nervous that I was enunciating all my words slowly. It was the only way I could get through a sentence without stammering.

"Well," he seemed kind of nervous, too. "I think my wife's having an affair."

"Oh, really?"

Got no Secrets to Conceal

My heart was really pumping. Of course, his wife was having an affair. I knew she was. I was the object of it.

"Yes, and I want you to find out if it's true. Would you be interested in doing something like that?"

"Uh, well, uh, yeah, I guess. Actually, I'd like to get a little more information before I commit. First of all, what specifically makes you think she's having an affair?"

"She stays out late after work a couple nights a week. Mondays she says she's working at Ramona's house. It's a part-time job she has up on Beach Hill. Her full-time job is with the county out in Watsonville. I believe she does go to Ramona's on Mondays. It's the Fridays that I'm worried about. That's her dancing night. Says she goes with a friend, Carol, but I'm not so sure. Especially after a weekend in June when I took our daughter on a trip to Arizona to visit Renata's folks, and I had a job interview. I parked in long-term parking at the airport on Friday. I tried calling her several times on Saturday night, and there was no answer. I even tried late, like three in the morning after the bars are closed, and still she didn't answer the phone. I think she spent the night with somebody, and I don't think it was Carol. Two Fridays ago, she said she was going dancing with Carol, but I called her number at about eight o'clock and she answered. I hung up as soon as I heard her voice. That's when I went to the Yellow pages and found your name. I didn't call you right away 'cause I didn't wan'a believe it, but then I thought about it and decided I had to know."

Jerome Arthur

He stopped there and didn't say anymore. I was speechless for the moment. That was the weekend of Renata's graduation. He seemed to have her all figured out. He knew the what; he just didn't know the who.

"So, what is it exactly you want me to do?"

"She's going out dancing this Friday. I thought if you could maybe follow her, see if that's really where she's going or if she's doing something else. You want the job?"

"Uh…uh, yeah," I stammered. "I charge a hundred dollars a day plus expenses."

He reached into his hip pocket and pulled out his wallet. He peeled off five twenty-dollar bills. I set my standard contract in front of him, and he gave it a cursory reading and signed on the dotted line. I wrote down the Boulder Creek address, which I already knew, and he told me she'd be leaving the house around six-thirty.

"That a bit early to go dancing?" I said.

"Says she's go'n'a meet Carol, and they're going out to dinner first."

"Okay, I'll take care of it. When you want me to report back?"

"How 'bout next Tuesday. I'll come back here while Tess is in preschool. Ten o'clock okay?"

"That'll be fine. I'm putting you in my calendar. Next Tuesday at ten. And I'll get on this right away."

So, there it was. Bill wasn't as open and tolerant as Renata was telling me. I guessed as much. I was having a crisis of conscience. When I was taking A.J. classes at Cabrillo, I swore that when I got my P.I. license, I'd never take domestic cases. And now here I was tak-

160

Got no Secrets to Conceal

ing a domestic case that I was in the middle of. My ethics were already compromised when I took the job; they were compromised when I climbed into the sack with Renata. Guilt was crowding me, but it dissipated as I looked at this new turn of events as an opportunity. Now I could find out if she was seeing other guys. I definitely suspected she was, but did I really want to know? The phone rang. It was Renata.·

"Hi, how are you?"

"Fine, how are you."

"Sorry I haven't called you sooner. Been hectic around here and at home. I've missed you and wanted to call you, but I've just been so busy."

"I've missed you too. Can we get together this week, like maybe Friday?"

I suggested it on purpose. I knew what her answer would be.

"I can't. Carol and I are going dancing."

"Aw." I tried to sound more disappointed than I was. "So, when will I see you again?" I said plaintively.

"Saturday afternoon when I finish doing some things for Ramona."

"Wan'a come to my place?"

"Sure. Is that going to be all right? I mean with Debra and all?"

"She'll be in San José visiting her parents," I said.

"I can hardly wait."

Twenty-six

Armed with my binoculars and Nikon camera, I drove up Highway Nine at around five-thirty on Friday night. I got to Renata's by six o'clock, and I parked on a side street that intersected her street. I couldn't miss her on her way to the highway. At six-thirty she drove by. I waited for just a minute before I pulled out. She'd already turned onto Highway Nine and was out of sight, but not for long. I made my left onto the highway and I could see her up ahead. There were two cars separating us, so I just followed. She turned onto Graham Hill and then Mt. Hermon Road. I followed her to Kings Village Shopping Center where she parked in front of a Chinese restaurant. I watched her go into the restaurant and walk to a window booth where a guy stood up as she approached. Before sitting down, she hugged the guy and he responded with a light kiss. I caught it all on camera.

I watched from my car as Renata and her date had dinner. They left the Chinese restaurant at about eight-thirty. They got into a Morgan roadster with the top down. She put a scarf over her hair and they drove off. I followed them to the Crow's Nest at the harbor. When they got into the restaurant's parking lot, he pulled up a few feet away from a Cadillac with two women dressed for the evening standing next to it. I went to the right in the lot and found a parking place one row over.

Got no Secrets to Conceal

A couple guys, who looked a little tipsy, walked over toward the Caddie, and one of them passed it and went up to the driver's side of the Morgan. He said something to Renata's date that I couldn't hear, and then he suddenly slugged the guy on the side of the head. The other guy rushed over to his buddy and pulled him away from the Morgan; he said something to him and pointed at Renata. Then they got into the Caddie with their dates and drove off. Renata's date pulled the Morgan into their parking space. I got a couple pictures of the two of them going into the Crow's Nest.

They were in the bar till almost nine-thirty. They came out and got into the Morgan and drove off. I followed them to a condo complex on Market Street next to Branciforte Creek. I got a picture of him pulling the Morgan into a garage. The garage door closed and that was the last I saw of them until a little after midnight when the garage door opened again, and they pulled out. I followed them back to Kings Village where they sat in the Morgan and kissed and hugged for a few minutes. I got more pictures of them in the Morgan. Renata then got into her car and drove home. When I was sure that's where she was going, I turned my car around and headed home.

I tried to be dispassionate, the consummate professional, but every time I saw them kissing, I felt like my insides were being kicked out. The whole two and a half hours they were in his condo, I sat outside stewing. So much for my being the only one for her.

I hit the sack as soon as I got home. In the morning I took a bike ride out to the Lane to look at the

163

waves. Communing with the ocean always helped me pull myself out of a funk. It would get me through that day. When I got back from the point, I waited till opening time at Bay Photo. I took my film in to get developed. What was I going to be doing with Renata later that day when she came to my place after Ramona's?

Twenty-seven

When Renata showed up at my place, she seemed friendly enough, but distant. I wasn't very friendly myself, and I was distant on purpose. Thoughts of the night before raced through my mind. She was wearing a new-looking T-shirt. I only mention it because I think it's the first time I ever saw her wearing a T-shirt. The logo on the shirt was a picture of a Volkswagen dune buggy. The business was an imported car repair service.

"How do you like it?" she asked, referring to the T-shirt. "This guy I went out with last night gave it to me. This is his shop."

"You told me you were going out with Carol last night."

"I knew if I told you what I was really doing, you'd get jealous and possessive."

I couldn't have been any more stunned than I already was from what I'd seen last night.

"Is he the guy fixes your car?" I asked.

"No. I met him at the Albatross a couple weeks ago when Carol and I did go dancing."

I nodded. Even though I knew what went on last night, I was still taken aback by her bluntness. And she didn't seem to mind telling me. She really wasn't telling me anything she hadn't already told me many times before.

"Last night wasn't even my first date with him. We had lunch at the Crepe Place earlier in the week. I went with him over to his shop afterwards, and he gave me the shirt."

I was so stunned that I couldn't say anything. I wanted to say *something*, fill the air with words. That way she couldn't say anything more, but I was paralyzed, and I lapsed into a brooding silence. My thoughts raced through a succession of her lovers. I imagined her making love to her ex-boss with the Dictaphone going, and then sitting down with the guy later and listening to it and laughing. Then I saw myself screwing her in a chair that afternoon of her college graduation. The obvious progression now was for her to do it with a grease monkey in the back seat of a Volkswagen dune buggy raised on a lift six feet up in the air. Why not? She said she needed adventure in her life. She'd once said that she'd never made love in a car. Well, I guessed this was her chance and she took it. She could have two "virgin rushes" at once: in a car and six feet up on a lift in a repair shop.

When I stole a glimpse of her in the mirror in my living room, I saw that she was watching me. There was a flicker of the June/July times in her eyes. She certainly was looking at me lustfully, but the look was alloyed with something else. It was rigidity so brittle that I thought her eyes would crack if she brought a smile to them. I'd seen that flintiness before, but I'd never seen it pointed so directly at me. I'd seen it when she talked about other people, like Bill when she was pissed off at him, or Leticia when Renata reached the point where she

166

had to assert her power over her. But now I was watching her look at me with those flinty eyes.

"I've got to get going here. Afraid I had too much to drink last night. A little hung over. Wan'a get home to be with my spouse and kid."

She'd been hanging with me for about an hour. I was also ready for her to leave. Better that than being caught between loving her and wanting to spend more time with her, and hating her (no, not hating, disliking maybe) and not wanting to ever see her again, and it looked like this last was how it would end. Her aloofness only increased my pain. I didn't understand how she could be so cavalier. Hadn't we experienced secret and mystical moments together? And when we weren't together, hadn't we sensed each other's needs and wants even when we were miles apart? At such times all it took was a simple phone call from one to the other, and we realized that we were both on each other's minds, and not just casually, but specifically with distinct feelings of a certain intensity. Yes, I was convinced there had been something very special between us, and I couldn't comprehend how she could dismiss it without a second thought. Yet as I gazed into her eyes, all I could see was brittle steel, as if those eyes were saying, "come on, quit being so maudlin."

When she left to go home (I *think* she was going home; I really didn't know or care at that point), I was left alone again completely mystified, but now I knew what I had to do. I knew that the relationship was over. I knew it last night. There was no way I was going to go out with her again. We weren't going to be lovers any-more. Now I had a job to do.

First thing Monday morning, I went out for a walk alone on Cowell's Beach. As I passed the Casa Blanca motel, I felt an oppressive sense of gloom come over me. We weren't ever going to get our room there again. Standing in front of the motel, I was hit by anoth-er sad memory of her. It was at this spot that I'd acci-dentally run into her that day two springs ago, when I'd hugged her for the first time and told her I wanted to go to lunch with her.

I walked up the hill past the Dream Inn and straight out the bike path to the point and back. I thought about her the whole time, my mind racing over the events of the past year until they became a complete blur. I searched out the positive moments and tried to use them to reinforce the thought that she loved me. As soon as I did, I was brought back to last night. No doubt I was just one among many.

When I got home, there was a message from Debra on my answering machine. She'd called before she went to work.

"Hi, honey. Wan'a go out to dinner tonight? Call me and let me know."

I was so agitated that I knew I couldn't see Debra right then, much less talk to her. I didn't want her to see me despairing as I was and start asking me ques-tions. I didn't call her back.

I went over to Bay Photo and picked up the pic-tures I'd taken Friday night. Then I sat down and wrote my report for Bill Lowell. I put in all the details I'd ob-

168

Got no Secrets to Conceal

served. Writing that report was like therapy. By the time I finished it, I was feeling much better, so I called Debra back and left her a message telling her to come to my place and we'd walk down to Riva on the wharf.

"Sorry I didn't get back to you right away after you called," I said when we met.

"How long was it?"

"Couple hours."

"That's nothing. I was at work anyway, so I didn't even know how long it was."

"Yeah, well, I wasn't feeling so good this morning and that's why it took me so long."

"Oh, honey! Are you okay? You feel better now? You don't sound well."

"I think I'm okay enough to do something. After dinner wan'a go for a walk out on West Cliff?"

I had to do something to keep from going crazy.

"Sure. It's Monday so Riva shouldn't be too crowded. We can get out of there early and go for a walk."

We went down to the wharf, ate dinner, and strolled along the beach.

"Why are you so distracted, distant?" Debra said as we walked. "What's wrong?"

I heaved a big sigh and said,

"I don't know. I'm depressed. Future looks empty."

"Are you having an affair?"

I was so taken aback by the question that I hesitated. That was all the answer Debra needed.

"You are! Aren't you?"

Jerome Arthur

"I'm sorry, baby," was all I could say.

"How could you do such a thing?"

I hung my head and cried, but Debra had no sympathy for me, and I didn't blame her.

"Am I ever disappointed in you! You broke my heart," she said through her tears and suddenly broke off. "Take me back to your place. I need to get my car and go home. I can't talk about this any more tonight."

We walked back to my cottage in silence. She didn't hug me before she got into her car. Instead she took off the engagement ring I had given her and handed it to me, and without another word she got in the car and drove off.

Twenty-eight

Tuesday morning came, and I hung out in my office after I'd eaten some breakfast over the morning newspaper. I had work to do, but I couldn't do it. I was so paralyzed, I couldn't do anything, and so I hung around and did nothing. Waited for Bill. Just a little over a month ago, I was in love with two women and they were both in love with me. Now I was still in love with both, but neither of them would have anything to do with me, and rightly so. I was a bum and Debra knew it. As for Renata's feelings, I think she saw me as just another john.

When Bill arrived, we sat down at my desk and I handed him the report. He read through it carefully, knitting his eyebrows and wincing when he came to parts that were painful.

"Wow! She really has been having an affair as I suspected!"

She was having at least two affairs that I knew of, maybe more. Her ex-boss was a possible (probable?) third. And who knew how many more.

I took the pictures I shot Friday out of the envelope and spread them out on my desk. It was then that Bill got an anguished, pained look on his face. Probably the same look I had on my face when I watched her through binoculars on Friday night and then again on Saturday when she couldn't wait to tell me all about it.

"Do I owe you any more money, you know, for expenses or anything?"

"We're good," I said. "I only put in a few hours on the job, and my expenses were negligible. Little bit of film. Some gas for the car. That's it. You paid me enough."

"Okay. Well, thanks. I don't know what I'm go'n'a do about this, but that's not your problem."

And with that, he was out the door.

He wasn't gone ten minutes when the phone rang.

"Hi," Renata said when I picked up.

"Hi, how are you?" I replied, trying to be as distant and aloof as I could be.

"I'm coming into town today. I have something to do at the county building. Wan'a meet me at the duck pond at twelve-thirty? We need to talk."

"I'll say! I'll be there."

I didn't wait for her to respond. I hung up the phone. It was eleven-ten. I had an hour and twenty minutes before I had to meet her. I dove into what I couldn't even think about before Bill got there. Now I got to work on one of the insurance cases.

I got to the park at twelve-fifteen. I wondered what she thought we were supposed to talk about. I had a good idea. She came from the direction of the county building parking lot and approached with what looked to me like resolve, and she didn't appear to be in a very friendly mood.

"I can't give you a hundred and fifteen percent anymore," she said after she joined me on one of the

Got no Secrets to Conceal

benches near the duck pond. "Your intensity is too much for me."

Boy, talk about getting right to the point. I didn't know what to say, so I said nothing.

"Once I was in a relationship with a guy I was really taken with. I didn't tell him how I felt for a long time, and when I finally did, he said it was a good thing I didn't tell him earlier because he would've ended it right then."

I had no idea why she was telling me this story again unless it was to wound me more than I was already hurting. She knew I didn't like hearing about her past lovers. Especially this one. The old ex-boss again, the one I was pretty sure was number three presently. Why was she bringing this story up now? I'd heard it before; I didn't need to hear it again.

"Since I last saw you, I talked to my mother on the phone," she said. "She was telling me it's easy for her to be with just one man, and not even think about any others. I haven't gotten to that place yet. Don't know if I ever will."

"So, I guess that means you're go'n'a be seeing guys other than me and your spouse?"

"Why does that bother you? It doesn't bother Bill. He's not proprietary like that. He's okay with it. Why can't you be?"

"I bet he isn't okay with it. I bet he gets jealous just like any guy would."

"You don't know him."

"That's right, and I hope I don't ever meet him."

This conversation was really getting weird.

173

Jerome Arthur

"I've got'a go," she said and abruptly stood up. I wasn't sure how we talked about so many things, but we did. The things we didn't talk about were what raced back and forth in my head. I wanted to scream. If I could just do that, I was sure my head wouldn't explode. The meeting ended all too soon (or not soon enough depending on point of view) with her telling me not to call her for at least two weeks and walking off without a backward glance.

I was hurting pretty bad, but I was clear now on what I had to do. Not only was I not going to call her in two weeks, but I'd also made my mind up that I wouldn't call her ever again. I was hurting, but I knew it would pass, and eventually I'd get over her and I wouldn't hurt anymore. A much more devastating thing for me now was the loss of Debra's love. She was the best friend I ever had and now she was gone. I called her about two weeks after we'd split up that fateful night on the beach.

"Wan'a get together and talk?" I said when she picked up.

"What's there to talk about?"

"Us and our future together."

"I don't think we have one, Jack."

"Ah, come on. I'm so sorry I hurt you. I won't ever do it again. I promise."

"Problem is I can't trust you. You still seeing your girlfriend?"

"Haven't seen 'er since before the last time you and I talked. She's out of the picture."

"Do you plan on seeing her again?"

174

Got no Secrets to Conceal

I wasn't expecting that question, and I had to think fast, too fast, and not fast enough. Debra caught my hesitation, but she didn't think twice.

"I think I want our relationship to be platonic. I just don't think I can trust you to be my lover, my husband, my man, and most of all, my friend. I love you, Jack, and I always will, but I can't live with you for the rest of my life."

I heaved a sigh of misery.

"Hearing you talk that way, baby, makes me so sad. I understand where you're coming from, and you're probably doing the right thing. I'm just go'n'a have to live with it, as hard as that'll be. Can we go out to lunch sometime?"

"Oh, absolutely. Give me a call next week."

"Okay, babe. I love you."

We broke the connection, and that was the last contact I had with her. The only time I saw her after that was when I'd run into her at Gilda's or the Santa Cruz Hotel or some other restaurant. We'd smile and say hello but that was all.

The End

1986-2019

About the Author

Jerome Arthur grew up in Los Angeles, California. He lived on the beach in Belmont Shore, a neighborhood in Long Beach, California, for nine years in the 1960s. He and his wife Janet moved to Santa Cruz, California in 1969. These three cities are the settings for his ten novels and one memoir.